Life Now - The Ultimate Life Framework

Life Now, Volume 1

Jim Pellerin

Published by Jim Pellerin, 2024.

LIFE NOW - THE ULTIMATE LIFE FRAMEWORK

First edition. March 25, 2024.

ISBN: 979-8224063369

Written by Jim Pellerin.

Also by Jim Pellerin

Life Now

Life Now - The Ultimate Life Framework
Invest Now - The Passive Approach to Winning at Real Estate

Real Estate Investing

Real Estate Investing Strategies: The Secret to Financial Independence with Real Estate
Real Estate Investing with Lease Options - Investing in Real Estate with No Money Down
Mastering REIT Investments - A Comprehensive Guide to Wealth Building
The Ultimate Beginners Guide to Real Estate Investing
The 98 Best Real Estate Investing Strategies
The Ultimate Beginners Guide to Wholesale Real Estate Investing
The Ultimate Beginners Guide to Rental Real Estate Investing
The Ultimate Beginners Guide to Fix and Flip Real Estate Investing
The Ultimate Beginners Guide to Private Equity Real Estate Investing
Ultimate Beginners Guide to Real Estate Investing Financing
Building Wealth Through Real Estate - A Beginners Retirement Guide
The Ultimate Guide to Marketing for Real Estate Investors
Unleashing Wealth: A Guide to BRRRR Real Estate Investing

Watch for more at www.jimpellerin.com.

Table of Contents

Life NOW

The Ultimate Life Framework

Jim Pellerin

Updated for 2024

Introduction

Chapter 1: Framework

I have been active in many different areas of interest throughout my life. I have had many careers.

I have a computer science degree. I have written 10 books on real estate investing. I was very active in sports, having been a gymnast, bodybuilder, and tennis player. I know a lot about nutrition and have lost a lot of weight fast. I have had several businesses. Some successful. Some failed. I know a lot about Internet marketing. I have raised several millions of dollars for various investment ventures. I have read over 1,000 books on personal development, business, sales, marketing, finance, investing, health and nutrition.

People kept telling me that I needed to focus. I always thought that there was something wrong with me because I was constantly thinking about all these different interests and even more. Then I realized something.

These interests are all related.

They are all intertwined. For example, it's hard to have a successful life if you are up every night watching television, eating pizza, and drinking beer. Now, maybe some people may see that the ability for them to be able to do that is a success. So if that's what success means to them, then all the power to them. But I don't think you are like them. Otherwise, you wouldn't be reading a book on how to live the *Ultimate Life*.

Part of living your *Ultimate Life* is determining what your *Ultimate Life* will look like. And it also has to do with understanding where you need the most work. What area of your life do *you* need to work on the most?

So what I have done is I have developed the *Ultimate Life Framework* that ties everything together. Here are the different areas of your *Ultimate Life* that you will need to focus on.

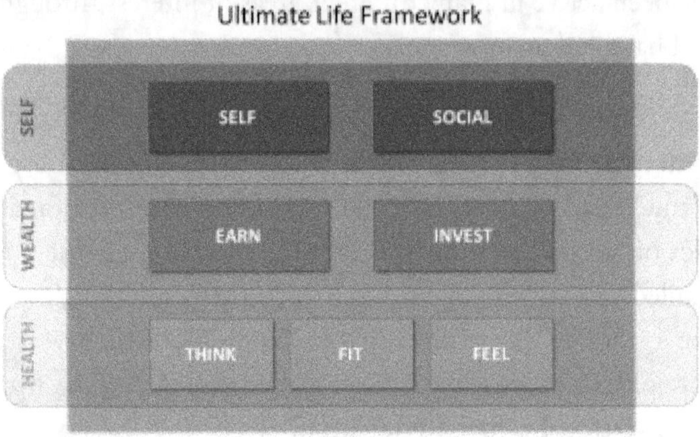

1. Foundation Stage - ***Health***

Your *Ultimate Life* needs a good foundation. This means you need to be mentally, physically, and spiritually fit. You need to work on your mind (think); your body (fitness); and your soul (feelings). You need to make sure that your body and mind are in tip-top shape and that you are putting the right fuel into them. Just like a car needs a good body and the right fuel.

<u>Think</u>: To be mentally fit you have to be careful about what you put into your mind. You have to be careful about what you read and watch on TV and make sure you are exposing yourself to the right information at all times. This is very tricky in today's society of social media, which is also where everyone seems to be an expert giving you their expert advice.

Fitness: How energized do you think you would be if you sat around and watched TV all day? That's what a lot of people do. They sit at their desk at work all day and then come home and plop themselves on their favorite chair in front of the TV or their computer or their phone where they surf *TikTok*, *YouTube,* or *Facebook*. You need to make sure you get a certain amount of exercise each day and that you are consuming the right *types* of food and the right *amounts* of food.

Feeling: How do you feel about yourself? Do you like yourself? Are you constantly putting yourself down or are you giving yourself gratitude regularly? Do you perform daily rituals such as affirmations? For some people that may also mean prayer or meditation. It's important to feed your inner self and to also treat other people with kindness.

2. Growth Stage - *Wealth*

The next area of your *Ultimate Life* is wealth. Wealth is about how you make your money and where you invest it.

Earn: what is it that you want to do to earn money? Some people want to be an entrepreneur and some people want to work for someone else. Either one is OK, as long as that's what you want to do. Running a business is a difficult thing to do and requires a lot of energy and business intelligence. Don't make the mistake of thinking you are an entrepreneur if all you are doing is the same work but with your own company name on it.

Investments: Most people today have no idea where to invest their money. The good news is that there are a lot of people out there who can show you where to invest your money. The bad news is that most of those financial advisors are broke. Do you want to invest in stocks, bonds, real estate, land, etc? There are lots of opportunities for you to do so. You need to take the time to understand what's available to you so you can make the right choices for yourself. Ultimately, you are looking for financial freedom.

3. Success Stage - *Self*

The final level of your *Ultimate Life* is how you think and act towards yourself and others.

Individual Self: What does success mean to you? This level of success is about achieving the ultimate level of success for YOU. It's setting the highest goals possible and achieving them. Have you ever heard of someone who is a multi-millionaire, who runs marathons every other month and is working on curing cancer?

You want to set your goals so high that you really have to stretch to achieve them. Not just lose 50 pounds, but place first in a local body-building contest. Not just earn $1M, but earn a salary of $1M and a net worth of $100M.

Social Self: What can you achieve socially? Are you an excellent husband/wife, father/mother, brother/sister, friend, member of society? Maybe you want to help out in your community or sit on a board of directors. What about social events? Maybe you want to be a member of a local social club. Maybe you want to travel. The alternative to all this is to sit at home watching TV, eating pizza, and drinking beer (FYI, I've done a lot of this when I was younger).

The concept behind this framework is that it's a lot easier to achieve your *self-goals* if you have reached your *wealth* goals and by practicing your *health* goals.

You may see a similarity between this framework and Maslow's Hierarchy of Needs. The big difference is that the *Ultimate Life*

Framework is more practical in its application as you will see in the next sections and chapters.

I also feel that you only have to focus on the areas where you need the most help. I guess this makes sense. But for those *specific* areas, you will need to make a much bigger effort so I am currently writing several books to help you with each specific area of the framework that I just mentioned.

Chapter 2: Your Ultimate Life

Life NOW

The User's Guide on How to Build Your Ultimate Life and Achieve Everything You Ever Wanted Out of Life.

Preface

Most people give up on life because they get lazy. They stop trying so hard. They become comfortable and complacent.

YOUR *Ultimate Life* will be different than anyone else's. It will be influenced by your wants, desires, and beliefs. It will be influenced by your upbringing and your social interactions. It will be influenced by your friends, your family, your business acquaintances, and all the other people around you. These people who have influenced your life in some way ... big or small. It could have even been a single event or a traumatic event that you experienced, but you didn't realize that it influenced you.

Your *Ultimate Life* may also be influenced by your *limiting beliefs* and the negative thoughts that you may have developed over the years as a result of the people and events who have helped influence you. Again, you probably don't even know that you have some of these limiting beliefs or maybe you know you have them but don't know how to get rid of them.

However, if you have limiting beliefs, those beliefs need to be identified and dealt with as part of your journey, and as soon as possible. Limiting beliefs can mean the difference between being a multi-millionaire and a bum. For example, what if you have been told all your life that *you would never amount to anything* and you now have a limiting belief that this is true? Becoming a multi-millionaire might be a stretch while having that belief.

When you set out to define your *Ultimate Life* for the rest of your life, it doesn't matter if you're 18 or 80. It just means you will have different goals and different activities. It is still *your Ultimate Life*. Someone who is 80 may not be able to become the head of surgery at a hospital, especially if they aren't even a doctor.

Your Ultimate Life is all about living your life without limitations so that you will achieve everything you want to achieve and be all that you were meant to be. To suck everything out of each and every day and to live life to the fullest.

Living your *Ultimate Life* means that your *actions* are congruent with your *thoughts*. It means that you will achieve results beyond your wildest dreams. Dreams that you never thought were possible. Well, at least, not until now. Because you are about to realize that anything is possible if you believe in it strongly enough and with enough conviction and purpose.

A lot of people go through life never realizing their dreams. They grow old with regrets. They die with their song still in them.

They live lives of quiet desperation.

What they don't realize is that it's not their fault. There are too many external influencers pushing them in the wrong direction. Influencers such as *society*, *education*, *diet*, and *exercise*. These wrong influencers cause decisions that initiate activities, and many times these are destructive activities.

At what point in their life did some people give up? At what point did they just say

I GIVE UP

Most people can't answer that question because it wasn't a moment in time when they made that decision. It was a gradual slip that slowly resulted in the situation. All those influencers took over and they just couldn't deal with it anymore. They got comfortable.

Life is what happens to you when you are busy making plans.

John Lennon

The following are just some examples of how people give up.

I'm going to be fat for the rest of my life. I'll just live with it.

I hate my job but it's a good job so I'm going to work there until I retire, then I'll enjoy my life.

I have a nice job making $40K per year ... that's all I really need.

Now, these people may not have actually said these things, or consciously admitted them, but somewhere along the line, a lot of people have made those decisions subconsciously.

I find it sad that people are proud of retiring. They are basically saying *I'm finally getting out of this job that I have hated all these years.*

I have seen a lot of people in these jobs who have coasted the last 5 or even 10 years, putting in the least amount of effort and with absolutely no job satisfaction

Alternatively, they could have pursued the career that they were really passionate about. The doctor becomes an actor, the lawyer becomes a rock star. There are countless examples of disgruntled employees who would rather be doing something else with their lives.

What I am referring to as your *Ultimate Life*, Ayn Rand, author in *Atlas Shrugged,* calls "an unrestricted existence". She said that this meant people can *do what they want, when they want, with whom they want, for as long as they want*, without limitations. I love this expression.

You should strive for this same level of life, this same level of success.

You only have one life to live. Don't waste it.

There are a lot of people who die with regrets about what they could have done but never did.

There are many reasons why people don't realize their full potential. The number one reason is usually fear. Although fear is sometimes disguised as complacency or obligation. *After all, I have a wife and kids to support now. I can't do that. What if I fail?* Sound familiar?

Another big reason for not achieving your *Ultimate Life* is that people are naturally lazy. It will take a lot of work and effort to live your *Ultimate Life.*

You will only get out of life what you put into it.

The biggest excuse I always hear from people is that they are too busy enjoying their life. They think that these mindless activities such as watching TV, internet surfing, social media, and playing video games are all part of life's enjoyment. But these are the same people who have the most regrets in their later years.

Let's begin your *Ultimate Life* journey.

Part 1: Foundation - Health

Introduction

Being healthy and fit is one of the most important prerequisites to having an *Ultimate Life*. Most people die before their time. They eat poorly. They don't exercise. They fill their minds with the wrong information which contributes to their limiting beliefs.

In this section, we are going to look at the foundational elements of the *Ultimate Life Framework*. They are the areas that I collectively refer to as *Health*. You must have a healthy foundation because without it your mind and body won't be able to function properly and you won't be able to achieve the things you want to achieve as part of your *Ultimate Life*.

The 3 areas or domains of life that make up this foundation are *Thought*, *Fitness*, and *Emotion*.

Thought is all about being creative and coming up with the plans that will help you work towards your *Ultimate Life*. It's about defining your *purpose*, *vision,* and *mission* and then coming up with the goals and plans to achieve your purpose, vision, and mission. I am constantly having to come up with new ideas and new goals for myself due to external influencers.

I have had the housing market crash in the middle of my previous real estate investment business. I had a total investment industry collapse while I was executing my business plan which cost me a lot. I had a real estate development project fail because of a local market shift and because of some bad people I had working for me.

So it's important to be able to think and plan and execute and to be able to change many times until you get it right.

The next component of the *Health* area is *fitness*. This is the one most people think about when they hear me talking about this *Health* area. Health is more than fitness, which I just mentioned in the previous paragraphs. And fitness is more than just physical fitness. It's also about mental fitness and emotional fitness. Mental fitness is making sure you are consuming the right information and staying away from all the negative information. You have been influenced negatively for long enough. It's time to start consuming the right type of information. Remember, negative information can contribute to negative or limiting beliefs.

You also want to make sure you are consuming the right types of food in your diet and the right amount of food. Most people eat way too much and eat the wrong foods.

The problem with diets these days is that there are so many of them and everyone has an opinion about which one is better for them. Go to a bookstore or search online for the words *diet book* and it will return thousands and thousands of books on the subject.

There do seem to be some basic diet principles that everyone now agrees on. Refined cabs are out. No more bread, pasta, pastry, and other refined carbs. Lean protein is a better choice. But people get into discussions about which type of protein is best. Is fatty better than lean? Should it be organic? There's the Keto diet, the Palo diet, and the Atkins diet ... just to name a few.

Next, you want to make sure that you are exercising regularly. You need a good mixture of cardiovascular-type exercises and weight resistance-type exercises. Most people think that if they take up jogging and cut calories they will get thinner and fitter. This is so not the case. Weight Resistance training will contribute more to your weight loss because you will be developing some good lean muscle which ultimately burns more calories over the long-term. Running or jogging only burns calories while you are doing it. Muscle burns calories long after you stop exercising for the day. Now you do have to work out regularly to maintain that level of fitness, but thats a good thing.

Exercising regularly also contributes to the overall health of your mind. Exercising releases endorphins which make you feel good and contribute to a positive attitude. It also contributes to your cardiovascular health. Your heart appreciates exercise, especially if you are at a level where you can exercise vigorously. And don't let age stop you. Healthy eating and good exercise will contribute greatly to your longevity. I have seen lots of cases where people are doing amazing things well into their 70s, 80s, and 90s. Check out *YouTube* for videos of *Arnold Schwarzenegger* and *Sylvester Stallone* exercising vigorously in their late 70s.

The good thing is that most people DO realize that exercise is good for them and they are more likely to engage in it.

The last thing we will address in this section is your *emotion*s or your feelings. How you think about yourself and how you treat others. It's about the relationship you have with yourself and with others. Are you a happy person? Do you treat others with respect? What do you do to achieve these feelings? Are you a spiritual person? Do you meditate? Do you practice affirmations? There are a lot of things you can do to feel good about yourself and the people around you.

There's an expression I like that I have always lived by. *It's not what happens to you that affects your attitude, it's how you react to those things that affect your attitude.*

Ever notice how some people can take just about any setback and keep on going? And for other people, you would think it's the end of the world if they get a flat tire. Shit happens. That's part of life. Don't sweat the small stuff and it's all small stuff.

I remember, during my darkest time, I was facing foreclosure, and repossession of my car, and my phone was getting cut off. I managed to resolve all those problems. But it was not by feeling sorry for myself or wallowing in self-pity. It was by accepting my problems and coming up with a solution for each. I pride myself on being a problem solver. Maybe I'm too good and I create problems for myself. Now there's a limiting belief. Ha ha.

So let's dive deeper into each of the 3 areas of *health.*

Chapter 3: Think

Section 1: Introduction

It's Not Your Fault.

What people may not realize is that what you think and do is influenced by a lot of external factors. You have grown up with a lot of influencers that have shaped your thinking and influenced how you react. Influencers such as your *parents*, your *teachers*, your *bosses*, your *idols*, etc. These people have all contributed to your beliefs and ultimately to your thinking and to the actions you take in life.

Most of the time these influencers have good intentions. They care for you so they are trying to offer you what they think is good advice that is meant to protect you and to help you. Sometimes these influencers can have an astounding negative impact on you. Such as in the case of an abusive parent or spouse.

What you put into your mind will impact all of your actions in life. Your thoughts and beliefs are the foundation of what you say and do and feel.

Garbage in = Garbage out

It's also important that you practice good mental health. This means knowing what to read, watch, and listen to. There's a lot of garbage out there that you are being fed every day. TV, radio, news, advertisements, etc. And now, with the massive adoption of Social Media, it's gotten even worse.

You should have a strategy for *how you think* and how it will influence your actions. You should try to practice empathy a lot more. How you think and feel about others is very important. Sometimes things aren't what they seem to be. In a lot of cases, you don't know the whole story.

In this chapter, I want to introduce you to a strategy that I have developed which is the result of me reading hundreds of books written by personal development experts and motivational coaches. People such as *Wallace Wattles*, *Napoleon Hill*, *Jim Rohn*, *Tony Robbins*, *Bob Proctor*, *Brian Tracy*, and many, many more.

It may not be your fault, but it's still up to you to fix it. Who else can you trust? You are in control. You are in control of how you react to something. You are in control of the decisions you make every day. So it's better to get in control of the right things to *think*, *say*, and *do*.

Everything that has happened to you is a direct result of something you have done or some decision you have made in the past. It's time you take back control of your life and stop blaming it on others or on things that might have happened to you in the past. The good news is that you can practice good mental health and make sure you have the most control over yourself.

The strategy I am about to introduce to you here is mostly based on the work by Wallace Wattles from his classic book *"The Science of Getting Rich"*.

In his book, he talks about getting everything you want in life if only you do things in a "certain way". I have added to his strategy and adapted it to be more pragmatic and practical so you can produce the results you want. Although his book is entitled *"The Science of Getting Rich"*, he does refer to the overall creative thinking that will allow you to "do, be and become" whatever you put your mind to.

His teachings go beyond just thinking about something and watching it appear, which is quite different from what *The Secret* teaches you. *The Secret* is a best-selling book by *Rhonda Byrne*. It is based on the belief of the *law of attraction*, which claims that thoughts can change a person directly. What you think about long enough and intensively enough, you will get.

Another famous book that focuses on thinking is *"Think and Grow Rich"* by *Napoleon Hill*. This is considered one of the greatest business books of all time. I have incorporated the concepts from both these books into this chapter as well.

In his book, *Wallace Wattles* stresses that *action* needs to be taken for your thoughts to become a reality. This strategy is quite different than what *The Secret* and *Think and Grow Rich* advocate.

The strategy I have developed is broken down into 4 distinct parts.

1. Purpose

What is your overall purpose for wanting something? This doesn't have to be your *purpose in life* but rather your purpose for wanting to do and achieve a *particular goal*. What is the *vision* you have for achieving this *specific* purpose? What are the attributes you need to possess to achieve this vision?

2. Goals

What are the goals you have to set that will help you in achieving your vision? These are short-term and long-term goals. You should have many short-term and long-term goals for each area of your *Ultimate Life*. Goals that cover all 7 domains. 30-day, 90-day, 1-year, and lifetime goals. All these goals must have dates assigned to them otherwise they are just dreams.

3. Action

Next, you want to identify all the plans and actions you can take to achieve these goals. These should be defined in as much detail as possible. You need to define all of the activities, milestones, and key results that you want to measure to monitor your progress. You also want to set dates for any short-term milestones.

4. Results

What are the results you will achieve by executing these plans and reaching these goals? What is the key objective or result of each goal? What is the main purpose of each goal? A goal should have a lot of "why" behind it. The greater the why, the greater the motivation, and the more likely you are to achieve your goal.

"Your beliefs become your thoughts,

Your thoughts become your words,

Your words become your actions,

Your actions become your habits,

Your habits become your values,

Your values become your destiny"

Mahatma Gandhi

In the next 4 chapters, I will go into more detail about each of these areas.

Section 2: Purpose

The term *purpose* is used a lot in self-help books. Some suggest that you need to develop your overall purpose in life and then do everything you can to fulfill that purpose.

The problem is that most people don't think that big. They have a hard time coming up with their *Ultimate Purpose*. One of the things you can do to determine your ultimate purpose in life is to write a list of all the things you enjoy in life. As you write that list try and monitor how you feel about each of those things. Did any of them make you cry or really hit you hard emotionally? If any of them did, then that might be your calling or your purpose.

Most people never really find out what their purpose is in life. Yes, others knew at a very young age and went on to follow their purpose and became very successful and very happy. *Al Pacino* has said many times that he believes he was put on this earth to act and to entertain people.

I believe you need to pick something as your purpose and then go after it. As long as it feels somewhat like a purpose. It's OK to change your purpose throughout your life. Several hugely successful people have pursued many different dreams. Look at *Arnold Schwarzenegger*. He has been a top bodybuilder, a top film star, and a top politician. And he always thought big.

You should also define a *purpose* for each of your goals. This means you would have several smaller purposes that would contribute to your much larger purpose that would motivate you for that specific goal.

For example, maybe you want to lose 50 pounds. Your weight loss purpose might be that *you want to feel better about yourself and don't want to be embarrassed when you have to go shopping looking for size XXL.*

Once you have decided on an *Ultimate Purpose* for your life, then you should decide on the *Ultimate Vision* you need to achieve to satisfy that purpose.

For example, I have had many purposes in life. In my younger days, my purpose was to have as much fun as possible. I think my vision was to party as much as I could. That's probably why I gained 50 pounds and got kicked out of university. I needed to change my purpose and vision or I think I would have ended up dead.

I did end up going back to university and receiving a degree in Computer Science. My purpose for getting my degree was to get a better job and enjoy a better lifestyle.

As I write this book, I have redefined my *Purpose* and *Vision* once again. I believe my purpose in life is to help others achieve their ideal life. Everything I have done, and everything that has happened to me, has prepared me for this new purpose. My *vision* in life is to help 1 million people change their lives by helping them create their *Ultimate Life*.

Millions of people are dissatisfied with their lives. They are in a relationship they don't want to be in. They work at a job they hate. They have lost the motivation they once had to be the success they once dreamed of becoming. I don't think anyone grew up wanting to be a bum or wanting to work in a dead-end job they hated. At what point did *you* become complacent? At what point did *you* give up?

You have been *drugged* into your current situation. Drugged with the teachings of all your influencers. Drugged by what you eat and drink. Did you know that sugar is more addictive than a lot of drugs? You are drugged by society and the governments and their beliefs. Go to school and get a good education and you will get a good job. Do you know how many people with degrees are working at fast food restaurants, or as cashiers, or other low-paying, unskilled jobs? Not that there's anything wrong with those jobs, if that's what you want to do.

And don't get me started on all the diet recommendations. You are constantly being bombarded with too many diet choices and too many bad food choices. But it's hard to know how to react because it's almost like you are being hypnotized. There is only 1 truth.

The only way to lose weight is to eat fewer calories than you burn.

Many people are aware of what they should eat and what they shouldn't, yet there are still a lot of overweight people in the world. The reason for this is not a lack of knowledge, but rather the fact that many of the foods we eat are addictive and often contain unhealthy carbohydrates. When you consume these foods, your body struggles to process them, and you may feel less motivated to exercise. Instead, you may find yourself craving more of the same comfort foods, like pizza or burgers and fries. Understandably, you enjoy comfort food, as certain foods can make you feel satisfied and happy.

In today's world, we are bombarded with an overwhelming amount of negative news and information daily. From war and terrorism to crime and deceitful behavior. It can be difficult to maintain a positive outlook. The media, including both traditional outlets and social media platforms, often contribute to spreading this toxic information. It seems as though staying optimistic is becoming increasingly challenging unless one chooses to isolate themselves from the outside world.

And that's what you have to do. You have to live in a virtual plastic bubble where you try and avoid all negative talk. I personally, never listen to the news or read it. I find it too depressing. And like *Mark Twain* said, *everyone complains about the weather but no one does anything about it.* So I never listen to the news because I can't do anything about it. Sometimes it's difficult to have a conversation with other people because I haven't heard about the latest crisis but I just tell them why. I get mixed reactions.

But I can have intelligent conversations about other things like diet and exercise, real estate, and other more important topics. There are lots of topics you can talk about without having to bring up some bombing in some country you've never been to or a shooting in a neighborhood where you don't live. I also don't listen to or check the weather because *I can't do anything about it.*

So, in summary, spend some time coming up with your *Ultimate Purpose* in life. Maybe you already know what it is but you are living a lie. Or maybe you are actually living it right now. Good for you.

The next step is to define your *Ultimate Vision*. This vision can be selfish as well, but it should be aligned with your purpose. For instance, if your purpose in life is to become an actor, your vision should not be to become the head of surgery at a local hospital. Unfortunately, many people's desires and actions are not aligned.

And finally, what is your *overall identity*? You can have several sub-identifies for each of the roles you have in life. For example, you might have a sub-identity as an *amazing dad, or lean mean fit machine, or CFO of your finances,* etc. But what is the *Ultimate Identity* that you want people to think of you as? What would you like to have carved on your tombstone?

My *Ultimate identity* is *I am an amazing Life and Business Coach* who has an *Ultimate Vision* of helping over 1 million people achieve THEIR own ultimate life and I am fulfilling my *Ultimate Purpose* of helping other people.

Section 3: Goals

"Whatever the mind can conceive and believe, the mind can achieve"

Napoleon Hill

Now that you have your vision in place it's time to set your goals. Your goals are generated through creative thinking. And these goals need to be aligned with your *vision* and *purpose*. The good news is that if you can *think* it, it can become real.

You can do anything, have everything, and become anyone you want ... if you want it bad enough.

There is a thinking stuff from which all things are made, and which, in its original state, permeates, penetrates, and fills the interspaces of the universe.

Wallace Wattles.

What you think about becomes a reality if done in a certain way. All things originate from thought. You have to think it before you can have it.

My problems all started when I realized I could have anything I wanted if I just wanted it bad enough and applied myself.

Specific Desires (Goals)

When setting your goals you need to be as specific as possible. You need to use the SMART goal-setting process.

<u>Specific</u> – be very specific and descriptive when defining your goals. *I want to lose 10 pounds in 2 months so I can feel better and fit into a size 34 pants.*

Measurable – quantify your goals. *I want to lose 20 pounds*, not *I want to lose weight.*

Achievable – your goals have to be achievable. *I want to lose 50 pounds in 1 month* is probably **not** achievable for most people.

Relevant – Goals should align with your *vision* and *purpose*. Ensure that pursuing the goal makes sense for your ultimate life. *I want to party 5 nights a week* may not be relevant for most people wanting an ultimate life.

Time-Bound – specify when the result(s) can be achieved. I want to lose 10 pounds *in 2 months.*

Beliefs

When creating your *goals*, you will be driven by your *beliefs*. These beliefs are the beliefs that have been formed over time by everything around you. Some of these beliefs will be *supporting beliefs* and some will be *limiting beliefs*. You will need to work on eliminating these limiting beliefs. How do you do this? By changing them.

How do you change them? One of the ways is reducing all the negativity that is in your life. This includes media, people, events, etc. Stop hanging around people who are naysayers and who always put down your ideas and tell you it can't be done, especially when they have never tried it themselves.

Stop exposing yourself to negative news and media. These sources of information can instill limiting beliefs in you. Instead, embrace positive and supportive beliefs that can inspire you to take action. Many people hold back from trying new things because they believe it's impossible. However, this way of thinking is often a result of their upbringing and education.

Thinking Habits

Once you set your goals you have to *feel* them. You want to create *emotion*. You have to experience them in your heart before they can become a reality. Create a strong mental picture for all of your goals. One of the things you can do is restate your goals every day, visualizing and feeling each goal. Get a success journal and start writing out your goals each day.

Faith

You have to have a strong desire for what you want and you have to *believe* that you will achieve what you desire. You must have *faith*. For example, if you want to be a millionaire, you must believe with all your heart that you will be worth $1M. You should see the $1M. Visualize it in your bank account. See the cheque that you get with one million dollars written on it. You could even experience what you would do with that million dollars.

This is also the *purpose* we talked about earlier. The *why* you wanted the $1M in the first place. Maybe it was to provide *financial freedom*. Maybe it was to provide *independence*. Maybe it was to *quit your day job*.

Experience in your mind what it would be like to not have to go to work every day and to stay home and spend time with your loved ones. Feel the fun you would have. See yourself playing with your children.

Luck is when opportunity meets preparedness.

Fears

Another thing you are going to have to learn to deal with and overcome is your fears. There are many types of fears. The *fear of failure*. The *fear of success*. The *fear of rejection*. The *fear of confrontation*. The *fear of performance*. The *fear of public speaking*, and so on. You have to discover your fears, overcome them, and do it anyway. *Just do it.*

Most of these fears are just your ego in action. You need to shed your ego and not worry about what other people think. And if you knew how little people thought about you, you would be insulted. If people aren't talking about you, you're not relevant. You can't please everyone. Now, I don't mean you have to be disrespectful or not be kind to people.

Fears can be overcome with practice and preparation. You need to be persistent in your practice. Repetition is the basis of a skill. The more you practice, the better you get at your craft. You are developing your skills and acquiring more knowledge. Eventually, you may become an expert which ultimately brings more confidence.

Discipline versus Habits

Discipline gets you started and habits get you to where you want to go.

You need to use discipline to stick with something until it becomes a habit. Some people say that it takes 66 days to build a habit. If you do something over and over again you are building habits. If you have a daily routine of getting up early, working out, and writing out your goals every day, you build that habit which will also build confidence in yourself.

Have you ever seen a gym at the start of the year? Their membership spikes in January. People will go for the first week or two. But eventually, they stop going. That's because they haven't built up a habit yet. They quit before their habit can be developed.

Section 4: Action

Now it's time to start taking action. Most people have ideas or goals that never come to life because they never take action. Or worse, they take action that is disjointed, incongruent, and unfocused.

When taking action, you need to act with intention. What that means is that your actions have to be aligned with your thinking and your goals.

In the previous section, we talked about your thoughts and about setting your goals. In this section, we are going to look at the actions you need to take to realize those goals.

A goal without a date is a dream. An idea without an action plan is also a dream.

I believe there are 3 types of goals that you need to set. There are *short-term*, *medium-term*, and *long-term* goals. Each of these sets of goals needs to be aligned with each other. You also need to set goals for all areas of your personal and business life. These goals all require action plans to be realized.

Remember to make sure each goal has a benefit, a reason, and a purpose. A person who has a goal with a purpose has a much better chance of achieving these goals. They are more emotionally involved.

Long-term goals are usually 5 years or more. These are very strategic goals. A 5-year goal may be *to be worth $10M in 5 years so I can retire and enjoy more time with my family*. The goal is *to be worth $10M*. The purpose is *to retire and enjoy more time with my family*.

Medium-term goals are usually 1 year. These goals are shorter goals that must be aligned with your greater purpose and also your *long-term* goals. So maybe a medium-term goal is *to be worth $1M in 1 year so you can leave your current job.*

Short-term goals are usually around 1 month. These goals are very tactical and include all the steps required to achieve these short-term monthly goals. These monthly goals must be aligned with your *medium-term* and *long-term* goals.

A short-term goal might be to set up a new company. Then you need to list all the activities you need to take to reach that goal.

This could include such activities as:

1. Create and register a new company

2. Develop a business plan

2. Develop a marketing plan

3. Create a new Website

4. Hire an Internet marketing person

5. Hire a salesperson

6. Create an initial prospect list

The more detailed the plan, the better.

Next, you need to execute the plan, all the while understanding that each activity that you perform is done with your ultimate purpose in mind.

Congruency and Focus

I talk to a lot of people who tell me they are busy and they have no time. These same people don't have goals or action plans. They think they are busy because they are doing lots of things but these *things* are usually activities that are NOT aligned with their goals or their thoughts and purpose. Your activities need to be *aligned* and *congruent* with your thoughts, desires, and goals.

When performing an activity, you need to stay focused on its completion. Do not allow yourself to get distracted or jump to another task. Some people think they are good at multitasking. There's no such thing as multitasking. Your brain can only work on 1 thing at a time. If you bounce around from task to task you are actually wasting time. Each time you start a task again you have to find out where you were before you left that task. These moments can add up and be overwhelming.

How much time do you spend on your activities? As much time as it takes to complete that activity in that time specified, or less. There is a law that states that *the amount of time required to complete a task will expand to the amount of time available to do that task.* So specify short concise time frames for each task.

Some activities fall into the category of daily recurring activities. What I like to do is create a collective goal for these activities. e.g. *Workout 5 days a week.*

So, once you have created your goals and identified all the activities required to achieve those goals you need to make sure you use laser focus to accomplish them. Do not let yourself get sidetracked from these activities. Nothing is more satisfying than keeping the promises you make to yourself. I have had lots of people in my life who never understood the commitment associated with goals. My favorite expression is about what I want from people.

I expect people to do things they say they are going to do when they say they are going to do them.

As I write this book I have set a goal of writing a minimum of 1,000 words per day. I expect this book to be 40,000 words, so that works out to about 40 days with more additional time for editing, formatting, and publishing. So the result is that I should have a fully published book within 60 days. As I check my word counter I see that I have completed almost 5,000 words in the first 2 days.

I do this because I know that I am most motivated and disciplined at the start of a project when no negativity or resistance has set in yet. I'm also working on the chapters that I already know a lot of the subject matter so I can write faster.

Having read over 1,000 books has provided me with a lot of background information over the years and does not require me to do a lot of research for these first chapters. One thing I have noticed when I read all those self-help books is that they are basically all saying the same thing. Like in my previous example, everyone knows certain things ... *if you want to lose weight, eat fewer calories than you burn.*

Most things in life are that simple. What holds people back the most is their *mental attitudes* and *limiting beliefs*. That's why I'm looking at all aspects of your life in this book and how they are related ... and they are ALL related. Mind, Body, Soul, Business, Investing, Individual and Social Self.

One final note about goal setting is that you want to set big outrageous goals that you may never achieve. For example, maybe your goal is to earn $100M in 10 years.

"Shoot for the moon. Even if you miss, you'll land among the stars."

Les Brown

Section 5: Results

Now that you have defined your purpose, created your vision, laid out your goals, and put together your action plans, it's time to *receive your results.*

"Relax", said the night man, "We are programmed to receive"

Hotel California by the Eagles

There are many types of *results* that you can *receive.* The results you receive will depend on the goals you create through your *creative desires* and goal planning.

Creative Desires

What you desire will come in many forms.

<u>Have</u> - What are the *things* you will receive or own?

<u>Do</u> - Where are the places you are *going to go* or the *activities you want to perform or do*?

<u>Become</u> - What is a new status you will receive (expert) or the new position you will obtain? What will you become?

*Before you can receive any of the results you want, you must be **ready** to receive them.*

A lot of people have done everything right but have never received their intended results. They defined their vision and purpose. Focused on the goals. They developed their plans and executed them with lots of energy. But they still haven't received their intended result. They worked really, really hard with no results. Or, at least, not the results they intended.

To receive the things you want in life, you must have an uninhibited desire.

What you don't realize is that your *life rules* may be stopping you from getting what you want. Your *limiting beliefs* may be inhibiting you. You may be sabotaging yourself because of your *fears* associated with obtaining a specific result.

For example, let's say one of your goals you have is to earn $1M. But you also have a limiting belief that all rich people are evil and that money is the root of all evil. You will never *receive your result* of $1M with that belief, no matter how hard you try. More focus, more visualization, and more activity cannot overcome a limiting belief like that.

To be able to receive what you want, you have to overcome your fears and your limiting beliefs. Some common fears are that you will be rejected; that you won't fit in; that you will lose your friends; that you will be a lot busier; that you won't have any time for yourself; and that you don't know what you are doing.

You may also be sabotaging yourself. Maybe not intentionally, but maybe subtly. So subtle that you don't even know that you are doing it.

You show up for meetings late. You miss appointments. You procrastinate. You don't return phone calls. You don't follow up. So what happens? You fail. This gives you great satisfaction because now you can tell everyone that what you were trying doesn't work. And you just move on to the next venture.

Most of the time you know what the problem is but you just don't want to admit it because it may mean you have to do something that takes you out of your comfort zone.

I remember for years I wanted to move up in this company I was working at. I wanted to be a manager. I liked the thought of being in control and making sure things got done. But the thought of having to stand up and speak in front of people scared me to death. I didn't want all the attention. I eventually got over it but I had to work hard at it. I took *Dale Carnegie* courses and actually took acting lessons. The scariest thing I ever did was the performance at the end of the acting course. All my work colleagues showed up to cheer me on.

So, how do you deal with those fears?

To overcome your fears, you have to face them head-on. You have to get rid of those limiting beliefs. You have to squash those inhibitors. How you do this is something you are going to have to figure out. It's something that only you can deal with but here are some tips.

The first thing you should do is write down a list of all the inhibitors that you can think of. For me, it was things like too much responsibility, confrontation, rejection, letting people down, and a bunch more.

A fear I always have is the fear that a certain task may take a lot more time than I originally expected.

Several years ago I had a major business fail. During that time, it consumed me. I was working 18 hours a day. I couldn't sleep. I had no time to myself. I ended up losing about $1M from that experience. The good news is I learned a lot. There are a lot of things I would have done differently knowing what I now know. The way I overcame that fear now is by making sure I have more people helping me so I can delegate a lot of the work I don't like doing to someone else.

Another common fear people have that they don't realize is that *they think they don't deserve the result they are trying to receive*. So they end up trying to sabotage themselves. How could someone like them, who grew up in poverty, expect to become a CEO of a large corporation or to be a professional athlete?

There are lots of examples of people who have overcome their limiting beliefs and negativity and have gone on to achieve the results they have always wanted.

The difference between a smart person who hasn't received the result they wanted and a person with a grade 10 education who is worth $10M and the owner of a very profitable business, is their ability to *receive*. They have removed those mental blocks.

"There has been much tragedy in my life; at least half of it actually happened."

Mark Twain

Results may come in many different forms. They may even come in a different form than was originally expected.

One person who wanted to be an actor ended up being a public speaker. Another person who wanted to be a doctor ended up being a life coach.

Once you start receiving the results you intended you should increase the level of *gratitude* to yourself. This will improve your positive thinking and may cause you to rethink your goals again. For example, let's say you made $30K one month and you have a new goal to make $100K. The first thing you want to do is express your gratitude to yourself. By doing this it will make you feel good and also provide input into your thought process, which increases the level of thinking for your continued goal setting.

Conclusion

In conclusion, this chapter has introduced a framework you can follow to achieve your goals. This framework consists of four parts: *Purpose*, *Goals*, *Action*, and *Results*. You first need to define your purpose in life and your ultimate vision. Then, you will set goals that are aligned with this vision. When setting goals, you should make sure they are SMART goals (Specific, Measurable, Achievable, Relevant, and Time-bound). You will also need to identify and overcome any limiting beliefs that may be holding you back. Once you have set your goals, it's time to take action. Your actions should be focused and congruent with your goals. Finally, you will receive the results of your efforts. However, to receive what you want, you must be ready to receive it. This means overcoming any fears or limiting beliefs that may be sabotaging you.

Chapter 4: Fitness

Section 1: Introduction

In this section, we are going to focus on your body and how it contributes to your overall *Ultimate Life*.

Today's business executives are also athletes. They usually participate in at least 1 sport and some level of regular fitness activity. They know that to work at the top level, they need a fit and healthy body.

In a previous chapter, we talked about the mind being fuel for the body. In this chapter, we will look at how food provides fuel and some fun for the body. Just like a car needs fuel, the body also needs fuel to run. The fitter you are, the more energy you will have and you will have a better outlook on life and business.

In this chapter, we will look at 4 areas of contribute to a more fit and overall healthy body.

<u>1. Mental</u> - To have to have a fit body, you have to want it. It's not just about you thinking you want to be fit, you must have a burning desire to become fit. Most people ignore this part. They try and push through their negative thoughts and think they can get to the gym just on sheer willpower. Like any other goal, you need a strong why and a strong purpose. Once you start working out regularly, you will develop a *habit*. This is when it becomes a lot easier. You no longer have to convince yourself to work out. It just comes naturally.

<u>2. Diet</u> - This is probably one of the most controversial subjects in today's society. For a long time, people have been brainwashed into eating the wrong kinds of foods. Carbs used to be thought of as

something good for you. And fats were supposed to be bad for you. That's why all these low-fat, processed foods were developed.

There was a lot of research done about the development of low-fat foods and they found out that when they took the fats out of certain foods, it was replaced with corn syrup or some other highly refined carbohydrate, to give it taste. By the way, another term for carbohydrates is sugar.

Refined carbohydrates are basically sugar. The more carbohydrates you eat the harder your pancreas has to work to secrete insulin to process the sugars and the more risk you have of becoming a diabetic. A couple of quick points: Fat doesn't make you fat. Carbs make you fat. Carbs that don't get digested get stored as fat in your body. And even though you might know that you are still eating the old way. This is a tough habit to break but you have to do it. See the *Mental* section above.

<u>3. Exercise</u> - This is yet another controversial subject. A lot of people think they know how to exercise but they don't. They lift too heavy or they lift too often. They do cardio to lose weight when they should be using resistance training to lose weight. Cardio might help you burn calories while you are doing it, but toned muscles will burn calories long after you finish training and make you look good too. Your muscles burn calories even while you are sleeping.

A good practice would be to incorporate both cardio and weight resistance training into your exercise program. Try a little running or biking with a little weight lifting and machine training. You can even combine the two by doing high-rep exercises with short rests between sets. You can start with simple exercises like push-ups, pull-ups, crunches, running on the spot, jogging, biking, body squats, or even something as simple as walking.

4. Other - Here is a list of things that are often overlooked when thinking about a good health and fitness plan.

Sleep - Sleep is one of the most essential things that contribute to a healthier life. Sleep gives your body a chance to re-energize itself and to get ready for the next day. How much sleep depends on the individual. Some people can get by with 5 hours of sleep, others need 7 or 8 hours. I think you should strive to get a minimum of 5 hours and a maximum of 6 hours of sleep per night. Again, some people can get by with less than 5 hours. I get between 5 and 6 hours. If you get more than 6 hours of sleep you are just cutting into your day.

Water - Water is essential to the proper functioning of the body. You must get at least 8 glasses of water per day. Water refreshes you and can cool you off. Water contributes to the proper digestion. Water lubricates your whole body.

Vitamins - You cannot eat enough food to be able to satisfy your body with all the vitamins and minerals it needs. I recommend supplementing your diet with an assortment of vitamins and minerals. The vitamins and minerals that you would need would be unique to your own body. It will depend on your sex, age, activity level, current health condition, past health condition, genetics, etc. I would recommend talking to your local pharmacist or someone who specializes in homeopathy-type medicine.

Medical practitioners - It's important to have preventive health care activities as well. This includes seeing your family doctor for regular health and medical checkups. You should also see your dentist regularly to make sure your oral health is good. If you wear glasses or contacts, you should also see your ophthalmologist regularly. Old prescriptions could cause headaches or worse accidents, especially if you operate a motor vehicle. I would also recommend seeing a chiropractor. Good spinal health is very important. Some people are scared to have their spine adjusted but I believe it provides overall benefits to your health and well-being.

There are a lot of things that contribute to good health. I will go into more detail in the next sections.

Section 2: Mindset

In this section, we will be discussing the mind again, but this time we're focusing on mindset from a *mental fitness* perspective. Just as your body requires regular training, you should also be training your mind regularly. It's crucial to maintain a positive attitude and constantly work on building your confidence and self-reinforcement.

What you put into your mind will greatly influence your thinking and your attitude. Your personal beliefs are a result of everything you see, hear, and do from your previous experiences in life.

There are several things you can do to help train and condition your mind. Here are a few.

Reading / Podcasts

It is important to expose yourself to materials that motivate and inspire you, such as books and podcasts. These resources can be motivational self-help books or educational books on a subject that interests you. However, be careful you don't fall into a trap. It is easy to spend too much time reading and not enough time taking action, which can hinder success. As an example, I used to read so much that I had little time left to complete my tasks. I have read over 1,000 books on various subjects. I still dedicate only about an hour a day to reading or roughly one book per week.

Seminars / Education

There are a lot of good seminars out there to choose from. Unfortunately, there are a lot of bad ones too. Many of these so-called seminars are free events where they get you into a room and try and sell you something. I'm not saying what they are trying to sell you isn't any good. I just don't like sitting through sales pitches to hear about something I can get online. Usually, the *free* seminars are more of a sales pitch than the *paid* ones.

Webinars / Youtube

I spend a lot of time watching webinars from various experts. The nice thing about webinars is that you can shut them down at any time if you don't like what you are hearing. I would recommend checking out some and seeing which ones motivate and inspire you. In some cases, it's almost like being live with them. Some people whom I have listened to are *Grant Cardone*, *Tony Robbins*, *Jim Rohn*, *Zig Ziglar*, *Gary Vaynerchuk*, *Brian Tracey*, *Dan Pena,* and a whole lot more. But again, don't get so consumed by these webinars that you don't have time to actually do any work.

Environment / Mastermind

As you go through life you will find that you may outgrow your friends. Assuming you are growing of course, which I'm hoping that everyone who is reading this book is interested in doing.

There's a saying that you are as smart and rich as the 5 people you hang around with. As you grow you will want to look for different people to hang around with. You will want to join certain clubs or societies where you can learn from people smarter than you.

If you are the smartest person in the room, you are in the wrong room.

You may want to join a mastermind group. A mastermind group is a group of non-competing professionals whose main purpose is the success of everyone in the group. There are different ways for these groups to operate but that is the basic premise.

Mentor / Coach

One of the best things you can do for yourself is to hire a mentor or coach. These are people who are either trained to coach you or who have been there and done it. I have used both. I have had about 4 or 5 coaches in my life. Most were good and a couple were OK. Coaches are there to give you direction and to provide accountability. They can help you get past your sticking points. They don't need to be an expert in your area of business. I think it's better if they don't know anything about your business. They can bring a different perspective and an objective viewpoint to what you are doing.

Journaling

One of the best exercises for your mind is journaling. You can start by keeping a journal and writing in it whenever you feel like you have something interesting to capture. One practice that people enjoy is writing their goals in it every day. Writing and re-writing your goals is an excellent way to reinforce them and keep them active in your mind.

Another thing you can write in your journal is gratitude. Write things that you are grateful for in your life.

Television / News / Social Media

There's a ton of bad information coming at you every day. You are exposed to thousands of messages from many different sources. Bad messages. Bad information. Negative information. It used to be that the sources of these messages were limited to TV and the Newspaper and more specifically the News. But now, with Social Media, it's everywhere. You should avoid all the negative information whenever possible. The way you can do that with social media is to avoid the people who are providing negative information. And the way you can do that is to unfriend these people or stay away from certain groups.

Naysayers

It's important to steer clear of naysayers who constantly criticize you or your pursuits. As someone who has been investing in real estate for more than 25 years, I've encountered numerous people who have warned me about the risks and potential losses associated with real estate investments. Interestingly, not one of these individuals had ever invested in real estate themselves. Generally, these naysayers are people who are close to you who mean well, and are just concerned about your well-being. They may also be trying to prevent you from becoming too different from them or more successful than them.

Affirmations

You should also come up with a list of affirmations that are specific to you and practice them daily.

Section 3: Diet

Your diet is one of the most important things you need to pay attention to. Your diet is responsible for providing the fuel for your body. A good diet can provide the right nutrition and provide you with energy. A bad diet can suck the life out of you, literally. It will make you tired and lazy. It will make you sick and cause life-threatening diseases. It will shorten your life. You need to take the time to learn more about nutrition so you can have a better life. The more informed you are, the better choices you can make.

There is a lot of controversy around what to eat and what a good diet is. The challenge is to pick something that's right for you. At the same time, there are certain foods that people all agree on that are bad for you.

There are a lot of diets and some of them are quite similar. I have adopted a lot of the principles from these diets. Some diets are very similar but with different names. I'm sure there are some specific differences. For example, there is the *Keto Diet*, the *Atkins Diet*, and the *Paleo Diet*. The one thing they all have in common is low or no carbohydrates.

Ketosis

I'm a big believer in converting your body from a carbohydrate-burning engine into a fat-burning machine. What this means is getting your body into a state of *ketosis*. What that means is reducing the amount of carbohydrate consumption to almost nothing so your body is forced to use the fat stores that you have accumulated in your body.

I'm not going to go into the details of what you can eat and what you can't eat but I will give you some specific guidelines. My favorite book on paleo and ketosis is *"Primal Body, Primal Mind: Beyond Paleo for Total Health and a Longer Life"* by Nora Gedgaudas.

Protein

My main food group is protein. I try to eat some protein at every meal. The controversy around protein is whether or not you should be eating high-fat protein or lean protein. I eat both but try to focus on proteins high in fat. The other thing you should do is try and eat organic protein whenever possible. Sure, it's going to be more expensive, but you're worth it. It's amazing how often I see people loading up their grocery carts with the cheapest food they can find and then heading off to the local store to get the latest video game.

Fat

Fat doesn't make you fat, carbohydrates do.

I remember when they used to show someone having a *good* breakfast. It consisted of whole grain cereal and some toast or a muffin and finished off with a glass of orange juice. A better breakfast would be high in fats and proteins. For example, I like to have a couple of eggs or an omelet. My meat is sausages, ham, or bacon. All of these are high in fat and protein.

Carbohydrates

The biggest killer of people is refined carbohydrates, or should I say *sugar*? Refined carbohydrates are very high in sugar. Carbohydrates are also highly addictive. Some people have said that sugar is 7 times more addictive than cocaine. Not sure if that's true, but it is addictive.

Whenever you eat a large amount of carbohydrates, you start to feel very sluggish. That's because your body and blood are working overtime to process that food. Your body secretes insulin to help process the carbohydrates you just ate.

Water

Another big item on your list of things that are good for you is water. A large part of your body is water so it only makes sense to drink a lot of water each day, but not too much. I recommend drinking about 8 glasses of water per day.

When I first became serious about losing weight I decided to change my entire diet. My current diet consists of high protein, a medium amount of fats, and almost no carbohydrates.

Intermittent Fasting

One of the techniques I use to lose weight is intermittent fasting. The way this works is that you don't eat for a large part of the day and only eat for a short part of the day. What I like to do is not eat from the time I wake up until around 5:00 PM. Then I have a meal at that time and something else in an hour or two. I do all my eating over 3 hours and do not eat again until around 5:00 PM the next day.

Some people say that breakfast is the most important meal of the day, so maybe they could get all their eating done between 7:00 am and 10:00 am and then fast the rest of the day. The nice thing about this schedule is you get to use your food for fuel to power you throughout the day.

I know there are some people out there who recommend the opposite of this approach. They recommend eating several small meals throughout the day. Do whatever works for you. I would recommend the fasting approach initially, especially if you are trying to lose weight. You can always change it after that if it's not working for you or if you don't enjoy it.

The only way to lose weight is to eat fewer calories than you burn in a day. You can easily measure the amount of calories because there are a lot of tools out there that can tell you how many calories there are in a piece of bread or whatever other food you are eating.

Another rule of thumb you can use is to never eat anything white. This means you don't eat white flour, white sugar, or white salt.

When I first started my exercise and weight training program I was a fanatic about it. I would train every day doing 1,000 reps a day. I would walk 10,000 steps. I would never eat a carb.

I know this works and gets you to your weight goals if you do everything right. But once you have lost your weight and have reached your ideal weight you can ease up a little. This means you can have a cheat day. Go ahead, order a hamburger and fries or a pizza. But for the rest of your meals, make sure you are eating right. This means you will keep your weight off, have more energy, and have a healthier life.

Your diet should be a lifestyle, not an event.

Too many people today confuse eating as fun. All their meals are supposed to be a happy occasion. That's because most people are addicted to sugar and seek the craving satisfaction from their comfort foods.

Section 4: Exercise

Starting an exercise program can be daunting, especially if you have never worked out before. But it doesn't have to be hard. I think most people overcomplicate their workouts and some people over-train.

The first thing you need to do is set your goals which you should have already done in your goal-setting in the previous Chapter of this book.

Your exercise program will vary depending on whether you want to lose weight or if you want to get in shape or both. And it should also be different if you have never worked out before.

Another variable would be whether or not you will be going to a gym or if you want to train at home. If one of your excuses is you can't afford to join a gym or you don't have time to go to a gym, then working at home can solve both those problems.

There are plenty of good exercises you can do that don't require weights or that can be done with simple bands or a couple of dumbbells. Also, by working at home, you save time by not having to drive to the gym and checking in and changing and all those time-consuming preparation activities.

The bad part about working at home is that you don't have anyone to look at to motivate you. The other bad thing about working out at home is that there are too many distractions. That's why it's important to create a habit out of training and include it in your daily routine.

There are 2 types of exercises that you will want to focus on. *Resistance training* and *cardiovascular training*.

Resistance Training - The best type of training you can do for weight loss is resistance training. That means weight training. When you workout with weights you burn lots of calories during the workout.

Resistance training usually increases your muscle mass. The more muscle you have, the more calories you burn on an ongoing basis. Cardiovascular training only burns calories while you are doing the workout.

Cardiovascular Training - The main reason you would choose to do some cardio training is to work your heart and improve your endurance and your cardiovascular ability. A common misconception is that people think cardiovascular training is what they need to do to lose weight. They go for a run or get on an elliptical and they work up a sweat and they relate that to weight loss. The problem with this approach is the weight loss benefits stop when you stop the exercise. Unlike resistance training where the weight loss benefits keep going *after* you stop training.

There are many ways to train and many body parts to train and many exercises you can do for each body part. The following is a program I recommend that helped me lose 20 pounds in 30 days.

1000 Rep Program

I would recommend the following program to start if you aren't already exercising. This program consists of 10 exercises x 20 reps, repeated for 5 sets each. 10x20x5=1000. I know it seems like a lot, but it's not really. It takes only 30 to 40 minutes to do. Repeat the workout for 30 days without missing a day or having a rest day. You are also trying to build a habit.

The goal of this program is to get your body used to exercising again without putting a big strain on it. To do 20 reps, you have to keep the weight for each exercise fairly light. The other benefit of this program is that it helps build up your endurance.

Exercises

The following are the exercises I did when I started my *1000-rep program*. You can modify these to suit your needs, depending on all the variables I mentioned earlier. If you aren't familiar with the exercise just search for it on the Internet and there are lots of videos and information on each exercise. I also had a home multi-gym that I used. I found it in an online classified ad. The guy who sold it to me delivered and set it up. The total cost was $300. Some of the exercises require the multi-gym.

1. Back: Lat Pull Downs: 20 x 5 (machine)
2. Chest: Seated machine press: 20 x 5 (machine)
3. Shoulders: Shoulder press: 20 x 5 (machine)
4. Legs: Seated leg press: 20 x 5 (machine)
5. Triceps: Straight bar push downs: 20 x 5 (machine)
6. Biceps: Dumbbell Curls: 20 x 5
7. Heart: Jumping Jacks: 20 x 5
8. Heart: Knee Raises: 20 x 5
9. Abs: Crunches: 20 x 5
10. Abs: Planks: 20 sec x 5

There are 3 basic ways you can include cardio training in your workout program.

1. Do cardio separately - Do your cardio training on a different day and keep it separate from your resistance training.
2. Do cardio between each set (e.g. do jumping jacks between each set).
3. Do cardio by reducing the wait time between sets, such is the case if you are doing giant sets.

I recommend doing the *1000 Rep Program* for at least 30 days and possibly 60 days. The goal is that you will stay on the program until you are bored with it and you feel like you can do more. The weights should feel too light and you are no longer tired at the end of each workout. You are also trying to build a habit when you are first starting out which is easier with lighter weights.

Push/Pull/Leg Split Program

The next program you want to jump to is a more traditional training program where you train certain body parts on certain days. You will be combining 2 body parts per day. The program and splits can vary, but I will include one here for you to try. You should try and do 3 to 5 exercises per body part. Here is the split.

- Mon: Chest/Triceps
- Tue: Back/Biceps
- Wed: Legs/Abs
- Thu: Chest/Triceps (repeat)
- Fri: Back/Biceps (repeat)
- Sat: Legs/Abs or Cardio (repeat or not)
- Sun: Heart (Cardio)

The way I like to train both of these programs is to do them in giant sets. So rather than do all of 1 exercise and then move on to the next, I will complete 1 set of 1 exercise and then move on to the next exercise until I have completed 1 set of all of the exercises in my program. Then I repeat the process 5 times. This can be difficult at a public gym.

The best time I have found to train is first thing in the morning. Your resistance becomes weaker at the end of the day so you may be more likely to skip your workout if you leave it until the end of the day.

Section 5: Other

When you think about fitness, you usually think about diet and exercise. There are a few other *fitness-type* things that you should be concerned with to make sure you are performing at your highest level.

Sleep

You have to make sure that you are getting enough sleep. There are many opinions on how much sleep is "enough". Some people say they need a minimum of 8 hours of sleep and others say they can get by with only 4 hours of sleep. And some people even like to sleep for 10 hours. I bet the person with 4 hours of sleep isn't working out every day or functioning at a very high level.

I think that 6 hours is all the sleep most people need. Any more than that and I think it just makes you lazy. Any less than 6 hours and I think you are sleep deprived and it affects your daily performance. But ultimately, it's still very specific to the individual. So try it out and experiment with different amounts.

The other key component to sleep is to try and get up early. Studies have shown that people who get up early are more productive and more successful.

If you are currently sleeping for 8 hours a day and you reduce it to 6 hours a day, you now have 2 hours more a day to do the things you want. Two hours a day x 7 days a week x 52 weeks in a year means you are awake for an additional 784 hours which is the equivalent of 43 18-hour days. Can you imagine what you can achieve with another 43 days a year? That's almost a month and a half. I always said that if I was able to get 1 wish in life, it would be that I didn't require any sleep.

One of the things you can do to augment your sleep is to start napping. You can take a nap in the middle of the day or when you think you need one.

So a complete sleep strategy would be to go to bed at 11:00 PM, sleep for 6 hours, and rise at 5:00 AM. If you are feeling a bit tired you can try and take a nap after lunch or after dinner. I find I can just cross my arms, close my eyes, and nap for about 15 minutes whenever I feel I need it.

Vitamins

There is no possible way for you to get all the nutrients and vitamins that you need just by eating food. You would have to consume a lot of food to reach the required doses for each of the needed vitamins. The following are, in my opinion, the minimal vitamins that you should be taking:

- Vitamin C
- Calcium
- B Complex
- Vitamin D
- Omega3

Medical Practitioners

The other thing you must do is make sure you are going for regular medical checkups. These include the following:

<u>Doctor</u> - Your family doctor will want to see you at least once or twice a year. They will usually want to do some tests for things like cholesterol or diabetes. Ask them to do as many tests as they can. The more information you have the better. It's better to be preventive than reactive. Most doctors react to symptoms. If you have a symptom, they

then decide what's wrong with you and prescribe a course of action. I prefer to be proactive and do as much as I can to monitor my health and fitness. So try and get them on your side and ask them to check for everything.

Dentist - Good oral health and hygiene are very important for your mouth and teeth. Lack of oral hygiene could lead to gum disease and tooth decay. Tooth decay that goes untreated could lead to losing that tooth. It also means your mouth has been exposed to some unhealthy decay for some time, which is also not healthy.

You can practice good oral hygiene by always brushing your teeth twice a day with good fluoride toothpaste. You should also floss regularly, which should be every time you brush and after every meal. Replace your toothbrush every three or four months. You also want to rinse with a mouthwash once or twice a day. Healthy teeth can make you look and feel better. And don't forget to schedule regular dental check-ups.

Eye Doctor - You want to have annual checkups with your eye doctor. If you need glasses, or if your prescription needs upgrading, this is very important. It's dangerous if you are walking around with old glasses with an old prescription. Especially, if you spend a lot of time in front of your computer which can cause eye fatigue. The wrong prescription can cause headaches and possible injury. Don't procrastinate on getting regular checkups and make sure your prescription is up to date.

Chiropractor - Some people swear by the use of a chiropractor and others get scared and won't have anything to do with them. I think a chiropractor is a worthwhile investment. A healthy spine is very important. You should start with an initial assessment where they will go over the condition of your spine. If you sit in an office all day chances are it won't be pretty. If you are fairly active you might be in better shape. After your initial assessment, you can start regular adjustments.

Initially, they may be quite frequent. When I first went I was going about 3 times a week. Eventually, I got to once a week and now once every other week.

This concludes the section on Fitness. Let's move on to the last part of *Health ... Feelings*.

Chapter 5: Feelings

Section 1: Introduction

Developing *emotional intelligence* can be an effective way for people to improve their overall well-being. Emotional Intelligence (EI) is a concept that can help individuals understand and manage their emotions, as well as navigate complex emotional situations with others. This idea is closely linked to Robert Plutchik's model of eight basic emotions. By using this framework for personal and interpersonal growth, individuals can gain a better understanding of how emotions shape their perceptions, actions, and relationships.

Emotional Intelligence: A Foundation for Personal Mastery

Emotional intelligence refers to a range of skills related to *recognizing*, *understanding*, and *managing* emotions. These skills help individuals develop a better understanding of their own feelings and how they affect others. People with high emotional intelligence are typically more aware of their own emotions and can better navigate social situations.

The four primary components of emotional intelligence can be categorized into two domains: **self-related** (*self-awareness* and *self-management*) and **social-related** (*social awareness* and *social skills*). The interaction between these domains forms the foundation for effective emotional intelligence.

Self-awareness is key to emotional intelligence. It means recognizing and understanding our own emotions. To be self-aware, we need to take a deep look at our beliefs, drives, and how we feel. It's not just about looking inside ourselves, but also being aware of how others react to us. This helps us to grow as individuals and become effective leaders. It also helps us to understand our strengths and weaknesses, and be humble.

Self-management is a part of emotional intelligence that involves controlling emotions and impulses. It includes things like emotional self-control, adaptability, and optimism. People with strong self-management skills respond thoughtfully to situations, rather than reacting impulsively. They are transparent and adaptable and can navigate challenges with resilience and positivity.

Social awareness involves understanding the emotional makeup of others. Characteristics of socially aware individuals include empathy, service orientation, and organizational awareness. These skills are foundational for building meaningful connections and effective interpersonal communication.

Developing good relationships is crucial in emotional intelligence and involves various social skills such as leadership, conflict resolution, and teamwork. People with strong relationship management skills are perceived as likable and can work well with others even in difficult situations. These skills are important for inspiring others, influencing them, and facilitating change. Those who possess these abilities can also help others develop their skills.

Robert Plutchik's Eight Basic Emotions

Plutchik's model groups emotions into eight basic types: *joy*, *sadness*, *anger*, *fear*, *trust*, *disgust*, *surprise*, and *anticipation*. These emotions can combine to form more complex emotional states. This model helps us better understand human emotions. It provides a good starting point for exploring the range of emotions people experience.

The Interplay Between Plutchik's Model and Emotional Intelligence

Emotional intelligence and Plutchik's model are closely related. Emotional intelligence involves identifying and managing the eight basic emotions in oneself and others. People with high emotional intelligence can understand and respond empathetically to other people's emotions, which helps to build strong relationships. Emotional intelligence also helps to control emotions and prevent impulsive actions that are caused by strong emotions like anger or fear. Skilled individuals use emotional intelligence to navigate relationships, build trust, solve problems, and communicate effectively.

Applications in Everyday

These frameworks find practical applications in different areas of life.

In *personal relationships*, understanding the nuances of emotions can enhance communication and create deeper connections. Emotional intelligence enables individuals to navigate conflicts with empathy and to find mutually satisfactory resolutions.

In *education*, acknowledging the role of emotions in the learning process can lead to more effective teaching strategies. Educators who are in tune with their students' emotional needs can create a positive and supportive learning environment, enhancing students' overall well-being and academic success.

In the *workplace*, emotional intelligence is increasingly recognized as a crucial factor in leadership and team dynamics. Leaders who demonstrate empathy and effective communication skills can inspire their teams, increasing morale, productivity, and innovation.

Challenges and Criticisms

It's important to note that the frameworks for emotions have limitations. Since emotions are highly personal and culturally influenced, it's hard to create a universal model. Additionally, there have been criticisms of the tools used to assess emotional intelligence, with concerns about their reliability.

Understanding and managing emotions is crucial for personal growth and healthy relationships. The combination of Robert Plutchik's model and emotional intelligence provides a comprehensive guide for achieving emotional mastery. These frameworks offer valuable insights into the complexity of emotions, interpersonal dynamics, and personal development.

Understanding how our emotions shape our thoughts, behaviors, and relationships can help us lead fulfilling lives and create meaningful connections with others. To navigate our complex emotional landscape, we can use tools like Plutchik's model and emotional intelligence. These resources can help us master our emotions and better understand the mysteries of the human psyche.

Let's explore this in more detail.

Section 2: Emotional Intelligence

As previously discussed, one of the things you can do to improve your overall feelings is to increase your *emotional intelligence*. In this section, we will dive deeper into this emotional intelligence.

Emotional Intelligence is the ability to understand your own moods and emotions and to understand the feelings and emotions of people around you. If you have a high emotional intelligence it means that you know how you are feeling, what your emotions mean, and how your emotions affect other people.

The 4 areas of emotional intelligence are areas related to yourself which are Self-Awareness and Self-Management; and areas related to others, which are Social-Awareness and Social Skills.

The following diagram shows these 4 areas and how they are related. I was unable to find the source of this diagram but the concepts are the ones widely accepted.

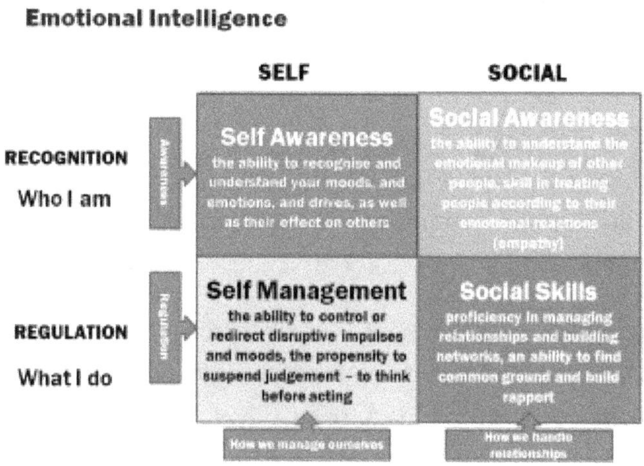

Self-Awareness

Self-awareness is about how aware you are of your own emotions and how accurately you can assess your emotions. Most of us are so busy that we hardly ever get a chance to think about how we react to our situations.

The other part of self-awareness is recognizing how other people respond to us. This is often difficult because we tend to see what we want to see and not what is really happening. We tend to avoid asking others for feedback.

Self-awareness is the ability to recognize and understand your moods, your emotions, and your drives as well as what their effect is on others. You need to know your own story and how it has affected you. You need to do this so you can make peace with your past. You should also know your *beliefs*, *emotions*, *behaviors*, and *relationship* patterns.

If you are self-aware, you will always know how you feel, and you will know how your emotions and your actions can affect the people around you. Being self-aware when you are in a leadership position also means having a clear picture of your strengths and weaknesses, and it means behaving with humility.

How to Improve Your Self-Awareness?

The following are some things you can do to improve your self-awareness.

Self-Reflection - To grow your self-awareness, consider building time into your day for self-reflection. Also, consider getting into the routine of collecting specific feedback from people who will be honest and whose ideas you value. People who seek out negative feedback are much more self-aware and effective than those who seek out positive feedback.

Keep a journal – Journals help you improve your self-awareness. If you spend just a few minutes each day writing down your thoughts, this can move you to a higher degree of self-awareness.

Slow down – When you experience anger or other strong emotions, slow down to examine why. Remember, no matter what the situation, you can always choose how you react to it.

Self-Management

Self-management is your ability to control your emotions. This component also includes your *transparency*, *adaptability*, *achievement*, and *optimism*. A key factor in self-management is whether you react or respond to situations. It is the ability to control or re-direct disruptive impulses and moods, the ability to suspend judgment and to think before acting.

The following are some characteristics of people with self-management.

Emotional Self-Control - Controlling your feelings and/or expressing them in the appropriate settings is a key skill.

Achievement Oriented - Being goal-oriented and being able to work toward your goals.

Initiative - Being self-motivated, and having the ability to keep working despite setbacks.

Transparent - being honest and open, interacting with integrity, and being trustworthy.

Adaptable - showing resilience and the ability to change course when necessary.

Optimistic - having a positive outlook, hoping for the best, and preparing for success.

How can you improve your ability to self-manage?

Know your values – Do you have a clear idea of where you absolutely will not compromise? Do you know what values are most important to you? If you know what's most important to you, then you probably won't have to think twice when you face a moral or ethical decision – you'll make the right choice.

Hold yourself accountable – Don't blame others when something goes wrong. Commit to admitting to your mistakes and facing the consequences. You'll probably sleep better at night, and you will quickly earn the respect of those around you.

Practice being calm – The next time you are in a challenging situation, be very aware of how you act. Do you relieve your stress by shouting at someone else? Try to do some deep breathing exercises to calm yourself. Write down all of the negative things you want to say on a piece of paper, then rip up the paper and throw it away. This is better than speaking them out loud. This helps you look at your reactions to see if they are fair!

Social Awareness

Social Awareness is the ability to understand the emotional makeup of other people. The skill of treating people based on *their* emotional reactions.

The following are some characteristics of people who are socially aware.

<u>Empathy</u> - one of the pillars of the ability to form connections with others, understanding and acknowledging others' emotions.

<u>Service Orientated</u> - being helpful, contributing to the group effort, and displaying good listening skills.

<u>Organizational Awareness</u> - the ability to explain yourself well and be aware of how you are being understood, as well as sensing the level of comprehension of your audience.

How can you improve your Social Awareness?

Put yourself in someone else's position – It's easy to support your own point of view. After all, it's yours! But take the time to look at situations from other people's perspectives.

Pay attention to body language – Perhaps when you listen to someone, you cross your arms, move your feet back and forth, or bite your lip. This body language tells others how you really feel about a situation and that the message you're giving isn't positive. Learning to read body language can be a real asset in a leadership role because you'll be better able to determine how someone truly feels. This allows you to respond appropriately.

Respond to feelings – If you ask a worker to work late – again, and although he agrees, you can hear the disappointment in his voice, respond by addressing his feelings. Tell him you appreciate how willing he is to work extra hours, and that you're just as frustrated about working late. If possible, figure out a way for future late nights to be less of an issue (for example, give him Monday mornings off).

Social Skills

Developing others, serving as an inspiring leader and catalyst for change, collaborating with a high-performing team, and managing conflict are part of relationship management.

You are high on this skill if others perceive you as likable and you're able to work well with diverse groups, even in the face of stress and conflict.

The following are characteristics of someone with good social skills.

<u>Inspirational Leadership</u> - you are a good mentor, role model, and authority figure.

Influence - you articulate points in persuasive, clear ways that effectively motivate others.

Conflict Management - you have the skills to improve relationships, negotiate, and lead. The ability to settle disputes, differences of opinion, and misunderstandings.

Change Catalyst - you recognize and support the need for change, and make it happen.

Developing others - you help others build their skills and knowledge.

Teamwork and Collaboration - you effectively work with others.

How can you build your social skills?

Learn conflict resolution – Leaders must know how to resolve conflicts between their team members, customers, or vendors. Learning conflict resolution skills is vital if you want to succeed.

Improve your communication skills – How well do you communicate?

Learn how to praise others – As a leader, you can inspire the loyalty of your team simply by giving praise when it's earned. Learning how to praise others is a fine art, but well worth the effort.

Section 3: Emotions

To have an *Ultimate Life*, you must be in control of your emotions. That does not mean you can't have certain emotions. It simply means that you are allowed to express those emotions when the time comes. You need to learn to attend to those emotions and express yourself through those emotions., Don't just disregard your emotions, but learn to recognize them and observe them. Become curious about your emotions, what caused them, and how they happened.

Don't be afraid to show your emotions in front of others and to share those emotions.

Emotions are an integral part of the human experience, shaping our perceptions, behaviors, and interactions with the world around us. As previously mentioned, Robert Plutchik proposed a comprehensive model of emotions that categorizes them into eight basic types. These emotions form the foundation of his influential psycho-evolutionary theory, providing insights into the complexity and richness of human emotional experiences. We will explore these emotions in more detail here.

Robert Plutchik's Eight Basic Emotions

1. Joy: Joy is a fantastic feeling that makes us happy and fulfilled. It motivates us to seek out enjoyable experiences and gives us a deep sense of well-being. We can experience joy in many ways, like spending time with loved ones, enjoying nature, or accomplishing a goal we've been working towards.

2. Sadness: Sadness is a feeling that comes from losing something or feeling disappointed. It helps us deal with tough situations. Sadness can range from feeling a little upset to feeling extremely sad and can cause physical and mental symptoms like crying or feeling tired.

3. Anger: Anger is a strong feeling that can happen when we feel threatened, treated unfairly, or frustrated. It can help us be assertive and tackle problems, but if we don't control it, it can lead to harmful behavior. Anger can be shown in many ways, from small irritation to big explosions, and it can make our body feel different, like faster heartbeats, tense muscles, and adrenaline rushes.

4. Fear: Anger is a strong feeling that can happen when we feel threatened, treated unfairly, or frustrated. It can help us be assertive and tackle problems, but if we don't control it, it can lead to harmful behavior. Anger can be shown in many ways, from small irritation to big explosions, and it can make our body feel different, like faster heartbeats, tense muscles, and adrenaline rushes.

5. Trust: Trust is important for relationships to work. It helps people connect and work together. To build trust, it's important to communicate openly, respect each other, and work towards common goals.

6. Disgust: Disgust is a natural emotion that helps us avoid harmful things. It can range from mild discomfort to strong revulsion and may cause physical reactions like nausea or avoidance.

7. Surprise: Surprise is when something unexpected happens and it makes you react quickly. It can be a small or big surprise, and you might show it by widening your eyes or gasping.

8. Anticipation: Surprise is when something unexpected happens and it makes you react quickly. It can be a small or big surprise, and you might show it by widening your eyes or gasping.

Plutchik's model further shows how these eight basic emotions can be combined to form even more complex emotions. For instance, *joy* and *trust* combine to create *love*, while *anticipation* and *joy* result in *optimism*.

To understand human feelings and reactions, we need to start by recognizing some basic emotions. This provides a foundation for exploring the complex world of human emotions.

Conclusion

Understanding and managing emotions is important for our well-being and relationships with others. Robert Plutchik's model of eight basic emotions and the concept of emotional intelligence can help with this. They provide a framework for categorizing and dealing with emotions in personal and social contexts.

Emotions shape our thoughts, behaviors, and relationships. It's essential to recognize and deal with them appropriately. These models are valuable tools for understanding our emotions better.

Section 4: Spirituality

Spirituality means something different for everyone. And the following are my beliefs.

First of all, spirituality means believing that there is something greater in this universe that is responsible for the universe. It's about faith. It doesn't necessarily mean faith in God, although that's what a lot of people believe in. It could just mean faith in something non-physical. Like a force that just exists that is there with you. To guide you. To protect you. Some people experience spiritual events by just enjoying a simple sunset or some other simple experience.

Spirituality is about how you feel when you are alone with yourself. Some people find deep spiritual feelings when they meditate, do yoga, go for walks, or do other calming activities.

Spirituality is how you experience things and how you treat other people. I knew some very religious people. They went to church every day and they prayed every day. But these same people weren't very nice. I don't think these people experienced spirituality.

Spirituality is all about your search for meaning and a deeper connection, kind of like a solo adventure to find yourself.

Religion, on the other hand, is like a club with shared beliefs and practices. While religion can be a great source of support, some people focus too much on it and forget that they have the power to make their own choices. Instead of saying things like *It's in God's hands,* it's important to remember that you can still take charge of your own life, even if you believe in something bigger than yourself.

To me, spirituality is about how you feel about yourself, how you feel about others, how you treat yourself, and how you treat others. It has nothing to do with following what others are doing or saying or going to church.

But there is a recognition that there is a larger force. In the books *Think and Grow Rich* and *The Secret* they teach you that you get what you think about. They suggest you are calling a *higher power*. There is a famous quote

You are what you think about all day long.

Emmerson

To make your dreams come true, it's not enough to just think about them. You need to align your thoughts and actions. There are many ways to do this, including praying, meditating, writing down your goals, and visualizing success. By actively engaging with your aspirations and believing in yourself, you can make them a reality. In previous chapters, we talked about different techniques to help you identify your desires and work towards them with intention. Remember, the key is to keep it simple, and always put the most important information first.

There is no right or wrong way to approach spirituality. What's important is to recognize that the journey is the prize so enjoy it.

Spirituality is about having a relationship with something non-physical that's bigger than yourself. Something that you can confide in in your times of need and in your times of joy. It's a belief that there *is* something bigger than yourself. It's a recognition of feelings and beliefs beyond your physical self.

Spirituality can contribute to increased levels of self-esteem, confidence, enjoyment, fulfillment, compassion, and many other feelings. It can also give you a sense of meaning and the value you provide in this world.

Being spiritual should also mean that you are acting ethically. This means that you do what is right and what you think is right. It also means that you do what you say you are going to do when you say you are going to do it. You are operating ethically. It also means how you relate to other people and how you treat those people.

An activity that could be linked to spirituality is performing affirmations. Affirmations are short sentences that reinforce what you believe in or what you want to believe. For example, an affirmation for someone wanting to be a good salesperson might be *I am the top salesperson on my team and I continue to set sales records every month.*

Some people need to achieve significance in their lives. This can mean many different things for each of us. For some, it could mean being a parent. For others, it could mean being the head of a company and for others, it could mean finding a cure for a disease. Whatever it is, you want to pursue the level of significance that makes you happy. The level of significance that is part of your *Ultimate Life.*

You should be living life with intention. You should have a sense of purpose. Why do you exist and how are you fulfilling your life's journey? Many people just let life happen to them with no direction and no convictions. They wander aimlessly through life until it's too late. Then they are left with regrets.

Your spirituality will have a big effect on your emotions and how you feel about yourself, how you react to situations, how you feel about other people, and how you treat other people. It's part of your *character*. It's what defines your personality and if you are a nice person.

This concludes the Foundation-Wealth stage of your *Ultimate Life*.

Part 2: Growth - Wealth

Introduction

The *Wealth* stage is an important part of your *Ultimate Life*. It's about earning and investing money wisely. This stage emphasizes creating a strong financial foundation through business ventures and diversified investments. In this article, we will explore the different aspects of the *Wealth* stage, detailing how individuals can use their resources to make money and ensure long-term financial growth.

1. Building Wealth through Entrepreneurship

Creating and Scaling a Business: At the heart of the *Wealth* stage lies *entrepreneurship* where individuals embark on the journey of creating and scaling their businesses, identifying market opportunities, and creating innovative solutions. Whether launching a startup or expanding an existing business, the focus is on generating substantial income streams through strategic business endeavors.

Strategic Business Planning: Ever wonder how your favorite stores or businesses keep growing? It's all thanks to something called strategic planning, which is basically a fancy way of saying they have a clear road map for success. This involves figuring out exactly what they want to achieve (their goals!), understanding who their customers are and what they want (market trends), and coming up with ways to keep getting better (like improving their products or making things run smoother). The ultimate goal? To make the business even more awesome and successful!

Income Diversification: Have you ever heard of income diversification? It's like having multiple baskets instead of just one for your eggs. By adding new products, selling to different customers, or partnering with other businesses, you can have multiple income streams. That way, if something happens to one of your baskets, you still have others to rely on. And who knows, maybe having multiple baskets can even help you make more money!

2. The Art of Making Money

Maximizing Earning Potential: In the *Wealth* stage, individuals focus on maximizing their earning potential. This might involve negotiating higher salaries, pursuing career advancements, or exploring additional income streams. The idea is to bring in more money than you spend so you can save and invest for the future.

Skill Development and Expertise: Acquiring specialized skills and expertise becomes a cornerstone of making money during this stage. Whether through education, professional development, or acquiring niche skills relevant to one's industry, individuals position themselves as high-value contributors, commanding higher compensation.

Financial Discipline and Budgeting: Financial discipline is like having a plan for your money. It's not just about getting a job, but also about being smart with what you earn. Budgeting is your tool for this plan. It helps you track your income (what comes in) and expenses (what goes out) so you can save and invest for your future goals and long-term retirement investments. Think of it as planting seeds now (saving) to grow a big, healthy money tree later (wealth).

3. Investment Strategies for Wealth Growth

Real Estate Investments

Real estate stands as a cornerstone of investment strategies during the *Wealth* stage. Individuals explore opportunities in residential and commercial properties, aiming for appreciation and rental income. Strategic real estate investments not only provide a hedge against inflation but also contribute to building a diversified investment portfolio.

Private Equity Investments

Investing in private equity allows individuals to participate in the growth of private companies. This could involve investing directly in startups or through private equity funds. While inherently riskier than traditional investments, successful private equity investments can yield substantial returns, contributing to overall wealth growth.

Retirement Accounts and Tax-Advantaged Investments

Strategic wealth growth involves optimizing tax advantages through retirement accounts such as 401(k)s, IRAs, or their equivalents. Individuals leverage these accounts to invest in a mix of stocks, bonds, and other instruments, benefitting from tax deferrals and compounding over time.

4. Financial Literacy and Continuous Learning

Embracing Financial Education The *Wealth* stage places a premium on financial literacy. Individuals actively seek knowledge about investment strategies, market trends, and financial planning. This commitment to continuous learning empowers them to make informed decisions, navigate complex financial landscapes, and adapt to evolving economic conditions.

Risk Management and Mitigation With increased exposure to various investment avenues, individuals at this stage prioritize risk management. This involves an understanding of risk-reward, diversification strategies, and the ability to avoid potential financial pitfalls. Prudent risk management safeguards assist in accumulating wealth and fostering long-term financial sustainability.

5. Legacy Building and Philanthropy

Creating a Lasting Legacy The *Wealth* stage extends beyond personal financial gain to include legacy building. Individuals think about the impact they want to leave on future generations. This might involve estate planning, establishing trusts, and creating a plan for passing on their wealth in a structured manner.

Philanthropy As people become wealthier, they often begin to consider philanthropy. This can involve making charitable donations, creating foundations, or supporting social causes. Giving back to the community is an important way to use wealth responsibly, and it has a positive impact on society.

6. The Role of Mentorship and Networking

Seeking Mentorship Having a good mentor has been key to the success of many wealthy individuals. Seeking guidance from experienced mentors can provide valuable insights, help navigate challenges, and accelerate personal and professional growth. Mentorship promotes continuous improvement and encourages learning from those who have already walked a similar path.

Strategic Networking During this stage, building a strong network is key. Think of it like making friends with people who can help your business grow. Your network could connect you with potential partners, investors, or people with great ideas. It's also a way to stay on top of what's happening in your industry, learn about new opportunities, and just get better at what you do.

In summary, the *Wealth* stage is basically about growing your money! It's where you take what you've learned and earned so far and put it to work even harder. This could involve starting your own business, finding ways to make more money at your current job, or investing your savings wisely. By keeping an open mind to new ways of making money and learning how to manage it well, you can build real wealth that will last you and even your family for years to come.

Chapter 6: Earn

Section 1: Introduction

You can get everything in life ***you*** *want if you will just help enough other people get what* ***they*** *want.*

Zig Ziglar

So what do you want to do with the rest of your life? You will need to answer that question at some time and it's never too late. You may change your answer along the way. I have changed the answer to that question several times.

How do you plan on earning money? There are many ways you can earn money. We will look at the *earning* type of income in this section and not the *investment* type of income.

There are 3 ways to earn money.

Employee - work for someone else

Self-Employed - work for yourself

Business Owner - others work for you

Employee

Most people earn money from a job as an employee. A lot of people who are working at a job wish they owned a business. If you own a business you could have a job or you could be a business owner. Confused yet?

There are many jobs available to you. If you have a *job*, you are an employee working for an employer. This can be very satisfying for a lot of people and not so satisfying for others.

Early on in life, you are asked to decide what type of job you would like to have and what type of career you would like to pursue. The problem with this decision is that there are many variables to consider.

Motivation: Obviously, you want to choose a career that you are going to enjoy doing. You want something that motivates and excites you. There's nothing worse than watching someone going to work each day at a job they hate, just waiting for retirement.

Income: Another influencer is how much will the job you choose compensate you. This is also a big driver for what a lot of parents are looking for, for their children. There are a lot of practicing doctors and lawyers who are in the wrong job. They follow their parents' desires and they end up in a job they hate.

Availability/Security: How secure is the job you are interested in? What's the longevity of that job? What happens when a job becomes obsolete due to technology, downsizing, etc? I have had to change jobs several times due to outsourcing, technology changes, and self-interests. I had to redefine myself each time.

So you have a big decision to make and hopefully, you make the right one.

Types of Jobs

There are lots of jobs to choose from. I'm going to classify these jobs into 3 basic categories.

White Collar: Takes place in an office. Professionals, doctors, lawyers, engineers, computer programmers, accountants, office workers, etc.

Blue Collar: Requires some type of manual effort. Tradespeople, auto workers, construction workers, mechanics, manufacturing workers, custodians, etc.

Pink Collar: Service-type work. Customer support, waiters, retail workers, entertainers, sales, etc.

Employees spend all their lives working for someone else hoping to retire and eventually have some time for themselves. *Earn* is about making money now, and on your own terms doing something you like NOW. And not having to wait for 30 years. One of the best ways to do this is to start your own business.

Business Owner

To become a business owner you will have to decide what type of business you want. There are many types of businesses to choose from.

Bricks and Mortar: This is a regular business with an office or store-front, with employees and lots of overhead.

Restaurant Owner: This is a specific brick-and-mortar business. A lot of people have opened restaurants because they like to cook. Most of these people are really just self-employed. Most gym owners end up in this situation as well.

Internet-Based: There are a lot of opportunities with Internet-based businesses. These are very popular these days because you can usually work from your home. This is a very popular business model.

Franchise - The problem with a lot of franchises is that you end up working **in** your business and you end up working a lot harder than an employee, in most cases. This means you are still self-employed. The good franchises are really expensive. At the time of this writing, a

McDonald's franchise requires a minimum of $700K in non-borrowed funds available to even apply.

Multi-Level Marketing – This is where you earn commission from the sales of a product and from the sales your team makes from the product. This requires you to sell the product and to sell the concept to others so you build a team. I think these types of businesses are very good opportunities for the right person. The main skills you need for this business are sales and marketing.

Activities

Most businesses require common activities that they must perform to stay in business.

Functional Activities: Businesses also have activities that are specific to the type of business they are in. This is the main function of a business. What does the business do? Make food. Deliver information. Manufacture products.

Marketing Activities: This is related to the promotion of the business and driving leads and interest in the products or services of the company.

Sales Activities: This is the activity of converting prospects into customers. Convincing the person that your product is the right one for them.

Operational Activities: These are the activities related to keeping the business going. These include human resources, financial management, etc.

Skills

All businesses require certain sales skills to be able to operate effectively.

Technical Skills: The main skill that the business is good at. Cooking. Repairing cars. Training people.

Marketing Skills: Skills required for marketing. Writing sales copy. Developing ads. Defining products.

Sales Skills: Skills required for sales. Building rapport. Asking for the sale. Closing prospects.

Computer Skills: As an online business owner, it always helps to have good computer skills. You will need some minimal computer skills to be able to do simple things like email and setting appointments. Computer skills also include being able to use mobile devices efficiently.

Stuck in a rut?

If you are in a job you don't like, you need to figure out how to get out. A lot of people get hired by a company. Then they start a family. They need security so they are afraid to leave that job. They get complacent and comfortable.

A lot of people are interested in starting their own business. But most people don't really know what that means and end up being employees for themselves as self-employed owners. These people spend too much time working *in* the business and not enough time *on* the business. Working *in* the business means doing all the function activities we talked about earlier. Working *on* the business is more about strategic planning, directing where the company is going, and hiring people to replace you to perform the day-to-day functional activities.

Passive Income

There is no such thing as passive income. There's a lot of misinformation out there about earning passive income. As a business owner, you will still need to be active in your business, to some extent. Especially in the early stages when you are still growing that business.

Section 2: Starting a Business

As previously mentioned, one of the most satisfying and rewarding things you can do is to *start a business*. Probably one of the most stressful and hectic things you can do is *start a business*.

Don't confuse being a business owner with being self-employed. If you can't leave your business without having it stop generating income, then you are not a business owner.

Self-employed people are *consultants*, *realtors*, *mortgage agents*, *taxi drivers*, etc. If they don't work, they don't get paid. In most cases, they are also responsible for doing all the overhead activities for their business. Things like accounting, payroll, marketing, sales, etc.

Being a real *business owner* means going from doing the *functional* activities of the business to doing the *management and growth activities* of the business. To truly be a business owner, with a growing business, you have to break away from doing the things that you were good at that made you want to start a business owner in the first place.

The baker has to become the *bakery owner*. The hairdresser has to become the *salon owner*. The Realtor has to become the *brokerage owner*.

Starting an *online business* can be a bit different because you can reduce a lot of the operational activities that you have to worry about. For example, you won't need an office. You may not even need any employees.

An online business may be different, but there are still certain things that all companies need to do.

Product or Services

What product or service do you want to offer? Do you want to develop your own products or promote and sell other people's products with *affiliate marketing*?

When starting an online business, I would recommend you start selling *affiliate products* that are closely associated with the product you want to eventually develop. This will give you time and money to be able to work on developing your own products and allow you to start making money quicker.

Marketing Strategy

How are you going to get people to find out about your product or service? Where will you market and advertise your product or service? What marketing systems will you put in place?

You will need to come up with a detailed marketing strategy that answers all these questions so you become crystal clear about what you are selling and how you are going to market your product or service.

Sales Strategy

How are you going to get your prospects to become paying customers? What sales strategies and systems do you need to implement? What sales scripts need to be developed? Who will be selling your products for you? What types of commissions will you be offering to your sales staff?

Operations Strategies

What systems do you need to put in place to run your company? How do you onboard your clients? How do you process payments? How do you provide customer service?

As an online business, you will want to keep these strategies as simple and as automated as possible. You want to keep your costs low and you don't want the cost of all this operational overhead to eat away at those profits.

Staffing

What staff will you need to help run your business? Do you need to hire people or can you *outsource* those activities at a cheaper cost? Don't make the mistake of thinking you can do everything yourself. When I was first starting in real estate I was the product developer, service provider, marketer, salesperson, accountant, property manager, etc. I even wrote my own contracts for all my real estate deals. There are some sites, such as *Upwork* or *Fiverr*, where you can go to outsource a lot of work.

Outsourcing

You can outsource everything from *admin* work to *marketing* activities and even *sales* activities. You have to be careful when outsourcing your work. You want to make sure you get quality work for a great price so you may have to try a couple of times before you find the right contractor.

The big benefit of outsourcing versus hiring employees, is you don't have all of the HR overhead. No payroll submissions, no tax submissions, no benefits, no office politics, etc. If you don't like the person, you just cancel their contract if it's a long-term contract. A lot of contracts can be time and job-specific. For example, you can contract someone to build a website.

Start-Up Capital

Raising *start-up capital* is a critical step in starting a new business, as it provides the financial foundation necessary to launch your new business.

Entrepreneurs must carefully assess their funding needs and explore various funding avenues, such as finding *investors*, applying for *loans*, or *crowdfunding*.

Crafting a compelling business plan that outlines the potential *return on investment* and growth projections is essential for raising money. Building a solid financial strategy and demonstrating a clear understanding of how the capital will be utilized instills confidence in potential investors and sets the stage for a successful start.

Hire the Right People

Building a competent and dedicated team is paramount to the success of any new business. The recruitment process should focus on finding individuals whose skills, values, and work ethic align with the company's vision. Entrepreneurs must not only assess the technical expertise of candidates but also their cultural fit within the organization. A cohesive team contributes to a positive work environment and enhances productivity. Investing time in thorough interviews, reference checks, and perhaps trial periods can pay dividends in securing a team that is not only qualified but also committed to the company's long-term objectives.

Focus on the Big Picture

Starting a business is exciting, but it's easy to get caught up in the daily grind and forget why you started in the first place. That's why it's important to keep the big picture in mind, even when you're dealing with everyday challenges. Think of it like this: having a clear vision of your goals is like having a roadmap for your business. It helps you make decisions that will move you in the right direction in the long run, even if things take some unexpected turns. By regularly checking in on your goals and making adjustments as needed, you'll be better prepared to succeed in the ever-changing world of business.

Build Relationships

In the business world, good relationships are just as important as having a great product or service. Talking to other people in your field, potential customers, and experienced advisors can open doors to all sorts of opportunities, like new ideas, partnerships, and even sales. By building a good reputation and being a consistent face in your industry, people will trust you and your business more. There are tons of ways to meet new people, from conferences to online groups. The real key is to make real connections, not just collect business cards. By building friendships with customers, suppliers, and anyone who matters to your business, you create a support system that will help you succeed for years to come.

Section 3: Marketing

Marketing is all about getting prospects interested in your product. But they have to find your product and find out all about it somehow. Your marketing strategy has to include a lot of different things and requires a lot of decisions and a lot of work.

Here are some of the marketing activities you and your team will need to figure out.

Product Type

What type of product or service do you want to sell? Here is a list of some online product types.

Information Products: I highly recommend selling information products. They have very little overhead and have no ongoing support. And once you develop it, it lasts forever. This type of product includes *courses*, *ebooks*, *webinars*, *manuals*, etc.

eCommerce Products: I use this name to differentiate from information products and to refer to selling physical products using online marketing techniques. This includes selling products from *Amazon*, *eBay*, *Alibaba,* and other physical product distributors.

eCommerce could also refer to you selling your own products. If you want to sell your own physical products you will have to deal with a lot of time-consuming activities such as shipping, inventory, returns, maintenance, etc.

Affiliate Products: This refers to selling other people's products. You become a *distributor* for someone else's products. The benefit is that you can start selling something right away without having to develop the product first. Commissions can be very good for some products.

This is a great way to start making money fast without having to spend any time on product development. You should pick a product related to a product you will eventually be developing and something you are interested in. For example, I'm currently developing real estate education and I'm also selling a real estate-based website affiliate product.

Product Niche

Now that you have picked a *product type* you need to pick a niche and a specific product within that niche. This "niche" is essentially a focused market segment with its own unique set of needs and interests. By catering to a specific niche, you can become a trusted expert and stand out from the crowd.

Finding Inspiration: Popular Niches with Proven Success

While there's no guaranteed "get rich quick" niche, some industries consistently perform well online. Here are a few examples to spark your imagination:

- **Finance:** Within *finance*, you could target specific niches like:
    - **Investing for beginners** - cater to young adults who are just starting to invest their money.
    - **Real estate investing strategies** - offer guidance for those looking to build wealth through property.
    - **Debt management solutions** - help people tackle student loans or credit card debt.
- **Health & Fitness:** This broad category offers endless possibilities. Here are just a few.
    - **Weight loss coaching for busy professionals** - tailor plans to people with limited time.
    - **Fitness routines for specific goals** - target niches like runners training for a marathon or people looking to build muscle.

    - **Vegan meal planning and recipes** - cater to the growing market of plant-based eaters.
- **Internet Marketing:** The online world is constantly evolving, and businesses need help navigating it.
    - **Social media marketing for local businesses** - equip small businesses with the tools to thrive on social media.
    - **Building effective email marketing campaigns** - guide businesses on crafting captivating email sequences.
    - **Content creation strategies for specific industries** - help businesses in a particular field (e.g., healthcare or fashion) create engaging content.

Remember, the Key is to Find Your Sweet Spot

While these are popular niches, don't feel limited! The ideal niche combines your interests and expertise with a market that has proven demand. Here are some questions to guide your search:

- What are you passionate about?
- What specific problems can you solve within your chosen category?
- Is there a community of people actively searching for solutions in this niche?

By combining your interests with a viable market need, you'll be well on your way to finding your online business's golden goose!

Online Presence

You will need to build an online presence to market and sell your product.

Imagine your online presence as your fancy online store! You don't need to build everything at once, take it slow and focus on what works for your business. Don't worry if you're not a tech whiz, hire other people who can help you set things up.

1. Your Main Store: Your Website

This is your main hub, like the storefront window for your product. People will visit your website to learn more about what you offer and to buy it. You can even set up a secure payment system here, just like swiping a card at a store!

Your website also helps people remember you - think of it like your brand's name tag.

2. Optional Bonus Rooms: YouTube and Social Media

These are like extra rooms you can add to your online store, but you don't necessarily need them all right away.

YouTube: If you're selling webinars or online classes, YouTube is a great place to show them off! Think of it like having a video screen in your store to show product demos.

Social Media: These are like busy streets outside your store. There are many platforms, but you can start small. Here's a quick guide:

- **B2C (Selling to Consumers):** Focus on *Facebook* and *Instagram*. These are like popular streets with lots of people walking by.
- **B2B (Selling to Businesses):** Focus on *LinkedIn*. This is like a professional networking event where businesses connect.

Remember, you don't have to build everything at once. Start with your website (your main store) and explore adding YouTube and other social media platforms as your business grows. If setting things up feels overwhelming, don't hesitate to ask others for help.

Online Advertising

Online advertising is using online services to advertise your product or service. To advertise properly you need to think about a few things first.

Target Market: Before you start any of your marketing activities, you have to define your target market. *If you are marketing to everyone, you are, marketing to no one.* The best way to define your target market is to create a *persona* of your typical customer. This should include everything from their *age*, *income*, *sex*, *job*, *relationship status*, *kids*, *interests*, *habits*, etc.

Messaging: Most business owners make the mistake of sending the same messages and the same advertising to all their prospects, regardless of where they are in their buying decision process.

There are at least 3 stages to a prospect:

- *Cold prospect*: These people don't know anything about your industry, what products are available, or what these products can do for them.
- *Warm prospect:* These people know something about the industry and they are looking for a solution and currently evaluating solutions.
- *Hot prospect:* These people have done their research and want more information about your product. Price and terms are the points of discussion.

Paid Ads: Paid ads in Internet marketing are essentially online advertisements that you pay for to reach a specific audience. It's like placing a sponsored message in a crowded online space.

Here are a few paid ad options:

- **Facebook Ads**: *Facebook* is probably the most effective advertising platform available today. The audience is huge. You can target your audience and the cost is reasonable. You can start with a very low budget.
- **Google Ads:** *Google Ads* lets you pay to show your mini-ads on Google searches and websites. When people search for things related to your keyword, your ad might appear, grabbing their attention and hopefully leading them to your sales page.
- **TikTok:** *TikTok*'s new paid ads let businesses create short, catchy video ads or partner with TikTok stars. This lets you reach a huge, engaged audience directly in their feed, perfect for boosting brand awareness and sparking conversation.
- **Other Platforms:** Social media sites like *Instagram* and *Twitter* offer ad options too. There are even paid ad networks for video platforms like *YouTube*, allowing you to showcase your product directly in front of potential customers watching relevant videos.

Webinars: Webinars are a great way of introducing your product to a prospect. Webinars can take someone from a cold prospect to a warm prospect. The key to a good webinar is to follow a defined process and script. The goal of a webinar is to convert the prospect into a buying customer or to get them to book a call if it's a *high-ticket* product. Lower-cost items can usually be sold directly from webinars.

Branding: Branding takes a long time. In the traditional way of starting a business, people used to think they needed to define their brand first. This meant hiring someone to come up with a name for your company and designing a logo around that company.

Modern branding activities usually include company name, logo, website, social media, blogging, videos, podcasts, etc. But you don't need to build a brand to start a business and you certainly don't need to do it at the start.

Collateral: Online businesses still need collateral. These can be electronic documents or can be printed material for in-person meetings if your business requires that.

- **Flyers**: Flyers provide a concise description of the benefits and features your product or service provides.

- **Presentations**: Contains similar information as a flyer but in more of a presentation style. There is usually a sales component to a presentation piece.

Email List: Email is *not* dead. One of the most important marketing things you can do for your business is to create an email list. Your email list will allow you to build an ongoing relationship with your prospects and customers. You should be using that list to communicate with your prospects regularly. The best way to do that is by using a piece of software called an *auto-responder*.

The way you add emails to your email list is by creating a capture page and offering a gift or lead magnet in exchange for them giving you their email. You can direct people to your capture page by running ads to it.

Section 4: Sales

If you want your business to succeed, you need to convert your prospects into paying customers. This can only be achieved through effective sales processes and skilled salespeople. Without sales, your business will not generate income and will not be sustainable.

Therefore, it's important to carefully plan your sales organization. Here are some factors to consider when setting it up.

Sales Process: The first thing you need to do is define your sales process. Sales starts where marketing leaves off. A typical sales process might include qualifying prospects, contacting clients, and closing clients. The better these processes are defined, the better chances you have of determining your company's income.

Let's say you get 100 prospects coming to you. You qualify for only 50 of them. Then you get on a sales call and find out only 10 of them are somewhat interested. Next, your closer gets on the phone and closes 5 of them. So in total, your sales process closed 5% of your total prospects. That can either be good or bad, depending on your industry and depending on the price of your product or service. Your sales process should be able to predict what that percentage should be.

Sales Scripts: Sales scripts can be very helpful when talking to prospects. They can help you follow a defined process. Be careful you don't sound too *canned* as it will turn off your prospects and have the reverse effect. I like to use a general script that directs what you have to say rather than one that has the exact words that you should say. This means the script is less prescriptive and sounds less contrived. A sales script is something that has been proven that you would give to all of your salespeople to make them more effective.

Appointment Setter: Appointment setters can be used to prequalify prospects. This leaves the actual sales to more experienced salespeople. Appointment setters usually get their prospects from marketing activities. You can also use online methods and tools to prequalify and set the appointments.

Sales People: Salespeople are a crucial part of your business. These are people whose sole job is to get your prospect to buy. You want to make sure these people are trained properly and are following your defined processes and scripts. A salesperson can take several months to sell big-ticket items. That means that these prospects will have to be nurtured during that period. You should have a good customer relationship management (CRM) tool set up to help the salesperson manage their prospects. Part of the process would be to make sure all activities are being logged and tracked in the CRM.

Closers: Some companies use a different person to close big-ticket items. These are highly experienced salespeople with several years of experience closing big-ticket items. They may even be a senior member of your company. I have had a lot of salespeople work for me over the years. Sometimes I would be brought in at the end to meet with the prospect and close them on the sale.

Compensation Plans

The key to having and retaining a good sales team is making sure you have a good compensation plan in place. You can use one or all of the following types of compensation in your plan.

Base Salary: This is a guaranteed salary that you give your salespeople, no matter how much sales they make. The point of this is to help take the lifestyle pressure off the salespeople so they can focus only on sales. Most companies require that enough sales be made to cover the base salary before the commission salary kicks in.

Commission Salary: Commission salaries are usually based on the number of direct sales. It is usually calculated as a percentage of that sale. For example, a 10% commission on a $10,000 sale would equal $1,000 in actual sales commissions. Some companies cap their commissions. I would not recommend doing that. What keeps the salesperson from leaving if he knows he cannot grow beyond a specified salary cap? Your salespeople should be the highest-paid people in your company. And you should be happy to pay them if they are making you lots of sales and money.

Bonuses: Bonuses are usually paid when a salesperson or sales team reaches a specified target or quota. For example, a 1% bonus is paid on a $1,000,000 target which would equal a $10,000 bonus. This is above and beyond the base and commission salary.

Residuals or Back-end sales: Some companies will pay their salespeople for commissions on other people's sales. This is very common in multi-level marketing businesses where the focus is on recruiting salespeople as well as selling their products. You may want to look at implementing a simple residual program that would pay commissions on any salespeople that your salespeople recruit. This would, of course, depend upon whether you are interested in having many salespeople. For example, you would pay 1% on all sales made by any salespeople you refer.

There are many different ways you can structure these compensations with many different permutations.

The tiered structure can be changed based on salesperson and company policies. For example, commission percentage and bonus would be increased if the base is eliminated.

Contract Sales People

When just starting your business, you may want to hire contract salespeople. This eliminates the need to deal with human resources and payroll issues. Some workers prefer this as there are some added tax benefits for them.

Lead Generation

Lead generating is not part of sales and should not be given to your salesperson. Lead generation and sales are 2 totally different skills. Don't waste your salesperson's time by giving them lead-generation activities as well. If anything, lead generation is part of marketing.

Customer Relationship Management (CRM) System

As part of your sales process, you want to make sure that you have a good CRM system that is used to track and manage your prospects. This will help your salesperson know where each of their leads are in the sales process. A good CRM will allow you to define the different sales and marketing stages right in the CRM. This will allow your salesperson to change their prospect's status as they move through their sales funnel.

The CRM can also be integrated with your auto-responder and could be used to send out automated messages depending on what stage the prospect is at.

Conclusion

A well-structured sales organization is fundamental to any thriving business. This section has explored the key considerations for establishing such a system, emphasizing the importance of:

- **A defined sales process:** A clear roadmap, outlining steps like lead qualification, client contact, and closing, ensures consistency and efficiency in converting prospects into customers.
- **Skilled and well-equipped salespeople:** Investing in training, and equipping your team with proper tools like sales scripts and a CRM system, empowers them to perform effectively.
- **A motivating compensation plan:** A combination of base

salary, commissions, and bonuses, tailored to individual performance and experience, incentivizes salespeople and fosters long-term commitment.
- **Clear division of labor:** Separating lead generation, a marketing function, from sales allows salespeople to focus on their core competency: closing deals.

By implementing these strategies, you can build a robust sales engine that consistently generates revenue and propels your business toward sustainable growth.

Section 5: Operations

Running a business requires a variety of daily tasks that are vital for its smooth operation and overall success. Other functions also contribute to the company's sustainable growth and efficiency. In this section, we'll explore these daily activities in detail.

Strategic Planning and Decision-Making

A successful business needs a good plan to guide its growth and adaptability. Creating a strategic plan is a process that goes beyond daily operations. It requires a thorough understanding of the market, competition, and trends. This involves examining the company's strengths and weaknesses, as well as the opportunities and threats in the external environment.

Market Assessment: To plan strategically, businesses must first analyze the market landscape. This includes studying consumer behavior, industry trends, and potential competition. By understanding the market's pulse, organizations can position themselves effectively, identify gaps in the market, and tailor their products or services to meet evolving customer needs.

Goal Setting: Setting long-term goals is an important part of strategic planning, and it serves as a guide for the organization. These goals help the organization know where it's headed and why. These goals could be about increasing market share, expanding to new regions, or introducing new products. Having well-defined goals makes it easier to make strategic decisions.

Risk Evaluation: When making strategic decisions, it's important to understand the risks and uncertainties involved. Businesses need to conduct thorough risk assessments to identify potential obstacles that may affect their goals. These obstacles could include financial risks, market volatility, or technological disruptions. To prepare for unforeseen challenges, a strategic plan should include contingency measures to mitigate their impact.

Expansion Strategies: When it comes to planning strategically, businesses need to consider opportunities for growth and expansion. This can involve entering new markets, diversifying product lines, or forming strategic partnerships. By identifying ways to expand, businesses can take advantage of untapped potential and strengthen their position in the market.

Competitive Positioning: Knowing where your business stands relative to its competitors is vital for strategic planning. This involves comparing yourself to industry rivals, identifying what makes you unique, and finding ways to gain a competitive edge. A clear understanding of your competitive position is key to making informed strategic decisions.

Financial management

Effective financial management is vital for a business to thrive long-term. It involves a variety of responsibilities that are crucial for maintaining financial health and making informed strategic decisions.

Bookkeeping: Keeping track of your day-to-day finances is crucial to managing them well. Bookkeeping involves recording all financial transactions, including income, expenses, assets, and liabilities. By keeping a well-organized ledger, you can gain a clear understanding of your company's financial position at all times.

Invoicing: Prompt and accurate invoicing is crucial for managing cash flow. Generating invoices quickly, specifying terms, and following up on payments are essential for ensuring a steady stream of revenue. Efficient invoicing practices contribute to the overall financial health of the business.

Budgeting: Budgeting is a vital aspect of financial management. It involves predicting income and expenses for a specific period, aligning financial goals with operational plans, and using resources carefully. Budgets act as guides for financial decision-making and resource allocation. By developing and sticking to a budget, you can make strategic financial decisions that align with your goals.

Cash Flow Management: Keeping track of the money that comes in and goes out is important for meeting short-term obligations and making the most of opportunities. A good cash flow management system involves tracking your income and expenses, managing what you owe and what others owe you, and keeping some money on hand for unexpected needs.

Financial Analysis: Regularly examining financial data helps to gain a better understanding of trends and patterns. Financial analysis involves evaluating key indicators of performance, profitability ratios, and liquidity metrics. This analysis provides insight that can identify areas in need of improvement, potential risks, and growth opportunities.

Payroll Management: Managing payroll is essential to ensure that employees are paid accurately and on time, while also complying with labor regulations. This involves calculating wages, taxes, and benefits, and then distributing payments to employees. Tax withholding and reporting requirements must be followed to ensure compliance.

Tax Compliance: Businesses need to follow tax regulations at the local, state, and federal levels. To do so, financial management is necessary, which involves keeping up-to-date with tax laws, filing accurate and timely tax returns, and implementing strategies to reduce tax liabilities. Ensuring tax obligations are met contributes to maintaining a business's overall financial integrity.

Financial Reporting: Regular financial reports can provide stakeholders with clear insights into a company's financial performance. These reports typically include balance sheets, income statements, and cash flow statements. Transparent financial reporting promotes accountability and helps with strategic decision-making.

Auditing: It's important to regularly audit financial records to make sure they're accurate. Audits are independent assessments of financial processes, internal controls, and compliance measures. They help build trust among stakeholders and identify areas for improvement.

Customer Service and Support

Exceptional customer service is crucial in today's competitive business landscape. It's not just a department, but a philosophy that should be integrated into every aspect of a company. Proactive customer service includes not only resolving issues quickly but also anticipating needs and exceeding expectations to build customer loyalty beyond individual transactions.

Responsive Communication: Effective customer service involves being responsive to customer inquiries through various channels, such as email, phone, and social media. By promptly addressing customer concerns, companies show they value their customers' time and contribute to a positive brand perception. It is important to communicate clearly and concisely, using simple language and short sentences. Organizing information logically and prioritizing important details can also help ensure effective communication.

Complaint Resolution: When customers make complaints, it's important to address their concerns quickly and with empathy. This not only helps to solve the issue but also presents an opportunity to turn unhappy customers into loyal supporters. To achieve this, it's important to listen carefully, understand the customer's perspective, and offer practical solutions. By doing so, the relationship between the customer and the brand can be strengthened.

Proactive Issue Identification: Good customer service involves identifying and resolving potential problems before they become bigger issues. This requires analyzing customer feedback and looking for patterns. By taking preventive measures, businesses can show their commitment to customer satisfaction and well-being. Identifying and solving issues proactively helps to create a smoother customer experience.

Maintaining Customer Databases: Keeping accurate customer databases is essential for personalized interactions. This involves tracking purchase history, preferences, and relevant customer information. By using this data, businesses can customize their offerings, promotions, and communication to meet individual customer needs and preferences.

Conclusion

In this section, we covered the crucial tasks that keep a business running smoothly and lead to its success. We covered strategic planning, which involves understanding the market, setting goals, assessing risks, expanding, and positioning against competitors. We also touched on financial management, which includes bookkeeping, invoicing, budgeting, cash flow management, financial analysis, payroll management, tax compliance, financial reporting, and auditing. All of these elements contribute to the financial health and long-term stability of a business.

In addition, we emphasized the importance of customer service and support in building long-term customer relationships. This involves responsive communication, complaint resolution, proactive issue identification, and maintaining customer databases to build loyalty and a positive brand image.

Overall, understanding and effectively executing these operations is essential for any business aiming to achieve sustainable growth and success. By seamlessly integrating strategic planning, financial management, and exceptional customer service, businesses can navigate the complexities of the market, solidify their financial standing, build strong customer relationships, and pave the way for long-term prosperity.

Chapter 7: Investment

Section 1: Introduction

If you have completed your *Health* and *Earn* objectives, it means you have reached a point where you are earning sufficient money to *Invest*. The primary objective is to invest your money in a way that enables you to earn passive income. If you opt for an investment that requires your active involvement, it will essentially be like taking up another job which will consume more of your time. That is NOT investing.

You will want to invest for many reasons. Maybe you want to build up your investment portfolio for retirement or to save for your children's education or both. The problem is that most people have no idea what to invest their money in.

Unless you work for a government or a large corporation, the days of companies offering pension plans are long gone. Most companies don't offer any type of retirement planning. If they do, it is usually that they will match your contributions in your 401K (USA) or your RRSP (Canada). This means that they leave it up to the individuals to manage their own retirement fund.

For some people this is good. For others, this is devastating. After all, you have a full-time job that you work at every day, a family to take care of and you are spending time trying to stay healthy and fit.

The following are a few investment options you can consider:

Stock Market

Why anyone would want to invest in the stock market is beyond me. They call it investing, but I think it's the biggest gamble people can make with their money. Most people choose to invest in the stock market because they consider it the easiest option for them. They think it's safe because the person selling these investments has been certified by the local securities organization after taking lots of courses. But in reality, investing in the stock market is not always safe and involves a considerable amount of risk.

It's important to keep in mind that most stock brokers or mutual fund dealers who sell you investments do not make as much money as you do, and they do not have any money invested in the investments they are recommending to you.

While there are many stocks to invest your money in, it can take a lot of time to learn how to make money there. It's worth noting that for you to win, someone else has to lose. This means you're essentially competing against large investment firms and more experienced investors. Even if you find a good broker, they will have the same challenges. Additionally, you may not have enough time to learn everything about your stock investment.

Another problem I have with investing in the stock market is that the market *perception* can change the price of a particular stock or class of stocks. This usually has nothing to do with the operations of a company. Usually, something may have happened outside the company that affected the price of your stock. Just look at what happens during a federal election or what happened during the Covid pandemic.

Stock market prices fluctuate on anticipated events as well as actual events. I don't know about you, but I would like to have more control over my investments and not be impacted by external events.

Mutual Funds

Mutual funds were created to help investors reduce their risk and make it easier to invest in the stock market. These funds diversify your investment by putting your money into different stocks and bonds that are in various industries, sectors, and locations. However, the issue with this strategy is that you are not truly diversified since you are still invested in only one asset class, which is stocks.

It is a common misconception that mutual funds are always a good investment option because they are traded by licensed professionals. In addition, many people mistakenly believe that investing in mutual funds provides them with more security because they are diversified. However, this is not necessarily true.

One significant advantage of investing in the stock market and mutual funds is that they are highly liquid. This means that you can sell your stocks and have the funds transferred to your bank account the very next day. There are even software programs available that can trade stocks for you based on a set of pre-defined rules. This is particularly popular among those who engage in *day trading.*

Day trading is a type of trading that involves high volatility and risk. In day trading, investors usually buy low-priced stocks, also known as penny stocks, that are available for less than a dollar. The goal is to sell the stocks for a profit within a day, hoping that the stock price will increase significantly. For instance, if a stock that costs $0.50 rises to $0.60, you can earn a 20% return on your investment in just one day. However, if the stock price goes down by $0.10, you will suffer a serious loss. Automated trading and day trading are very risky and require extensive knowledge and resilience to succeed.

Savings Accounts

Savings accounts are seen by some people as an investment option.

Many people find it frustrating that the interest rates on savings accounts are so low. It is not uncommon to see interest rates ranging from 0.5% to 1.5% for savings accounts, which is a far cry from the double-digit interest rates that were common in previous decades. If you invest a significant amount of money, like $1,000,000, you will only earn a meager $5,000 to $15,000 for a year. Considering the current cost of living and the high inflation rate, this return on investment is hardly enough to make a substantial difference in anyone's financial situation. It is understandable why people may feel frustrated with such low-interest rates, as it can feel like they are putting their money into a bank account for no real benefit.

Guaranteed Investment Certificates (GICs)

GICs are a type of long-term investment that you can make with banks. When you invest in a GIC, you are essentially lending money to the bank, and in return, they pay you interest on the loan. The bank then uses your money to provide loans to others, such as mortgages and personal loans.

Banks typically offer a higher rate of return on GICs compared to savings accounts. In the current market, the interest rates on GICs typically range from 1.5% to 2.5%.

Other Investments

So now that I've bad-mouthed the stock market and savings accounts, in the next sections let's look at investments that make better sense and aren't as scary as you think.

Real estate, *private Loans*, and *equity investments* are by far a much better investment. They will make you more money and are less risky. There is this misconception that some of these investments are riskier than the stock market, but that just isn't so. The risk is not doing your homework and investing in the wrong investment. The exact same thing happens with the stock market.

Conclusion

While the section highlights the challenges of navigating investment options, it emphasizes the importance of building a secure financial future through **diversification and careful planning**.

Traditional methods like savings accounts may offer low returns, and the stock market, while potentially lucrative, carries inherent risks. It's crucial to remember that **not all investment options are created equal**, and understanding your **risk tolerance and financial goals** is paramount before making any decisions.

The section encourages readers to **conduct thorough research and consider seeking professional guidance** from qualified financial advisors to explore a broader range of investment possibilities beyond the ones mentioned. This may include exploring **alternative investments** like real estate, private loans, or equity investments, which, when approached strategically, can provide potentially **better returns and reduced risk**.

Remember, investing is a journey, not a destination. By **educating yourself**, **diversifying your portfolio**, and **consulting with professionals** when needed, you can make informed choices to achieve your financial objectives and build a secure future for yourself and your loved ones.

Section 2: Real Estate Investing

So what is real estate investing anyway? This is a loaded question with lots of answers. The quick and easiest answer is:

Real estate investing is investing in anything real estate related.

There are many ways to make money in real estate and I will cover the most common ones here.

Rentals

Most people are familiar with rental properties as a preferred method of real estate investment. This involves purchasing a property and renting it out to tenants. Your profit is the difference between the income you receive from rent and the expenses you incur. Rental investing is a long-term strategy, particularly if you're investing in single or small multi-unit properties. This is due to the high expenses required to maintain these properties. Expenses such as *mortgage payments*, *taxes*, *maintenance*, and *property management fees*.

The real money in rental investing comes from the *appreciation* of the property value over time as a result of the price increase of the property, and the *principal paydown* of the mortgage as a result of the regular mortgage payments.

This strategy can be a mostly passive investment if you can find a competent property manager and if your rental income covers the expenses. It's important to ensure that you at least break even.

You could also invest in much larger rental complexes but this would require you to partner with someone who has more experience and to help out with the financing. These investments can be highly profitable or quite costly.

Fix and Flip

This is another popular strategy because of all the programs that are on TV these days. The challenge with this strategy is finding the right properties. The right properties are the properties that are severely undervalued and they don't require a huge amount of money to fix them up. These properties are hard to find but they are out there. There are a lot of risks with this type of investment strategy.

The first one is that you may have underestimated the amount of work and therefore the costs required to renovate the property are much higher than you had originally estimated.

The next risk is that the house might not sell for the price you wanted it to sell for so your profit is reduced and you could suffer a loss if you have to sell it at too low of a price. This happens to people who don't know the market price for houses in the location they are buying in.

The third risk is that it takes longer to sell than you had originally thought. This means you have to *carry* the property for a longer period which would cut into your profits and might even end up losing you money. Usually, you will have to pay for such things as mortgage payments, utilities, taxes, etc while you are waiting to sell your property. Also, don't forget to factor in the cost of a Realtor when you do the initial financial analysis.

Fix and flips can also be very time-intensive if you have to spend too much time managing the project yourself. You should make sure that you find a good contractor with a good team so you can make money with as little involvement as possible. Don't expect to make a profit on every deal too. It may take you a couple of deals to learn the strategy before you start making money with fix and flips.

Lease Options

Another less common, investment is a lease option or rent-to-own investment. This is where you have a property that you rent to someone and they have the option to buy the property they are renting. The advantage of this strategy is that the *tenant-buyer* is much better than you would get with a normal rental tenant.

You can also get your tenant-buyer to do all the maintenance and repairs in this strategy. A big advantage of this strategy is that you make money in 3 different ways. Once at the start when they give you what's called an *option consideration*. Next, you get paid *monthly rent* and you can dictate the rent and subsequently, the profit you want your tenant-buyer to pay you. And lastly, you make money when your tenant-buyer *purchases* the property at the end of the lease option term.

The disadvantage of this strategy is that you must look for properties at the end of the lease option term because the tenant-buyer should have purchased the property if everything goes as planned. Check out my book on *Lease Options*. It's available on Amazon and other major bookstores along with all my other books.

New Development

Developing a new house is not a very common strategy. It is usually left to the larger professional developers. This method involves purchasing a piece of land and constructing a house on it. This can be a profitable venture, provided that the land and construction costs are lower than the value of other properties in the same area. It is also possible to construct multiple townhomes on a single piece of land, maximizing the per unit cost of the land for each unit's development.

If you are considering new development, make sure you choose a reputable developer. Be firm about your costs and try to avoid unexpected expenses. Experienced developers, who are familiar with the area and city by-laws, permits, and inspections, can help you with this.

It is always a good idea to hire a *Realtor* to sell your finished project. They can provide valuable assistance with listing, staging, and showing the property. If you are in a desirable market, you may not need to hire a realtor and can sell the property yourself. You could even *pre-sell* the unit if the market is right.

The profits from this venture can be quite substantial, as you are building the property for cost and keeping all the profits for yourself, without any middlemen other than your Realtor.

Section 3: Loans and Mortgages

Loans and Mortgages

Investing in loans and mortgages can be an effective way to grow your money. Essentially, you act as a lender for other people's real estate projects, such as development, fix-and-flip, or long-term rental projects. This means that you function in a similar way as a bank. There are multiple ways to lend money, which depends on your risk tolerance and familiarity with the borrower and the project.

Mortgage

A *mortgage* is a type of loan that is secured against a property by placing a lien on the property. As a lender, you are similar to a bank, providing a loan to the owner of the property which is secured by the property itself. The loan will have similar conditions to those of a bank-issued mortgage, such as a specified term, interest rate, and amortization period.

As an investor or lender, you may consider providing an interest-only loan from the borrower. This approach simplifies the payment process for both parties and results in more consistent and lower payments for the borrower. Alternatively, you could request a standard blended payment mortgage that includes both interest and principal. Another approach is to request a balloon payment, whereby the borrower must pay back the entire original loan amount and all the accrued interest on a specified date.

There may be other mortgages secured by the same property as your mortgage. For instance, the property owner may have received *traditional financing* from a bank, which means they already have a mortgage from the bank. The bank always wants to have their mortgage registered on title in the *first position*. This ensures that if the borrower defaults, they will be paid first. The second position is a *second mortgage*, which means it's the second mortgage to be registered on title. This mortgage will only get paid after the first mortgage is paid if the borrower defaults. The second mortgage typically has a higher interest rate because of its higher risk position. This is where an investor usually positions themselves with their mortgage.

Another way to put money into a project is to be one of the *owners* of the property and to hold a title position on the property. To facilitate this arrangement you would usually have a *joint venture agreement* that would spell out all the terms and agreements of the partnership. This would cover such things as who pays for what and how the profit is split at the end of the project and after the sale of the house.

These terms and conditions must be properly understood and agreed to before the project starts. Make sure you hire a lawyer to draw up the joint venture agreement and who is experienced with these types of agreements.

I have seen a lot of projects fail because each party thought the other party wasn't doing their fair share. There is usually a *money partner* and a *project partner*. The money partner tends to be a silent partner and lets the project partner manage all the project parts of the project. If the money partner sees that the project isn't going so well, they may step in and ask for some changes or offer to assist in some way.

Loans

Another type of investment could be a straight-up loan to the owner of the project. This is usually done this way if the investor is very familiar with the owner and the type of work that he will be doing. Another reason for doing this is because the bank does not allow a second mortgage to be placed on the property.

Instead of a mortgage agreement, there would be a *Promissory Note* signed to seal the deal. The note would specify all the terms of the loan similar to the terms of a mortgage and joint venture. The note could still show the property as collateral but the lender would have to sue the borrower to get his money back if the project doesn't go well or if the borrower doesn't pay the lender at the end of the project.

When you hold a mortgage or you are part of a joint venture, the lender is automatically entitled to payment when the property is sold. This payment is made from the funds generated by the sale. There is also a private market for the buying and selling of these notes, which provides lenders with some degree of liquidity if they wish to exit the deal early. Essentially, they can sell their note to another investor, although it will usually be at a discount.

The mortgage and the promissory note come with a pre-defined fixed amount of profit, expressed as an interest rate. The joint venture profit will depend on the amount of profit the project makes and the terms of the joint venture that dictate how much percentage of the profits each party gets. The advantage of the joint venture approach is that the investors could see a lot more profit than the mortgage lender. The disadvantage of the joint venture is that the investor could see a lot less than the mortgage lender. There is more risk in the joint venture arrangement but it also comes with a potentially higher return.

The last type of loan investment could be a simple loan to someone for something other than real estate. This could be a loan to purchase a car or some other asset or even to start a business. If you are contemplating this type of investment loan you should always make sure you have some type of collateral. As shown, the most common and best collateral is a mortgage on an existing property.

One thing to remember when using a property as collateral is to always make sure that the property is worth more than the loans that are secured by the property. The lower the amount of mortgages on the property, the lower the risk. The ratio of the loans to the property value is referred to as the loan to value. You should probably stay away from lending money for a property that would result in a greater than 80% loan to value (LTV).

Section 4: Private Equity

Private equity investing has become a popular way for investors to earn better returns and be more involved in growing businesses. Unlike public equity markets, private equity involves investing in private companies that aren't listed on stock exchanges. This section explains the basics of private equity investing, its benefits and risks, how to get involved, and important things to keep in mind when investing in this unique area.

Definition and Structure

Private equity represents investments made in private companies, ranging from startups to well-established enterprises. These investments are typically made by private equity firms, which pool funds from institutional investors, high-net-worth individuals, and other sources. Private equity is characterized by a longer investment horizon compared to public equity.

Types of Private Equity Investing

Private equity investments operate using various types of investing:

1. **Venture Capital**: Involves investing in early-stage startups with high growth potential. Venture capitalists provide funding in exchange for equity ownership.

2. **Buyouts:** This entails acquiring a controlling stake in a mature company, often to restructure, optimize operations, and drive growth. Leveraged buyouts (LBOs) involve financing the acquisition with a significant amount of debt.

3. **Mezzanine Financing:** This represents a hybrid form of financing that combines debt and equity. Mezzanine investors receive interest payments and equity warrants, offering a higher risk-return profile.

4. **Exit Strategies:** Private equity investors realize their returns through exit strategies, such as selling the company, taking it public through an initial public offering (IPO), or merging it with another entity.

Benefits of Private Equity Investing

1. **High Return Potential:** Private equity investments have the potential to deliver higher returns compared to traditional asset classes

like public equities and bonds. This is attributed to the active involvement of private equity firms in the management and strategic direction of portfolio companies.

2. Diversification: Private equity offers diversification benefits by providing exposure to a broad range of industries and sectors. This diversification can enhance a portfolio's resilience to economic downturns and market fluctuations.

3. Operational Influence: Private equity investors often play an active role in the management of portfolio companies. Their strategic input and operational expertise contribute to business growth and value creation.

4. Long-Term Horizon: Unlike public markets, private equity investments are typically held for an extended period, allowing investors to participate in the long-term growth and development of portfolio companies.

Risks and Challenges

1. Liquidity Risk: Private equity investments are illiquid, meaning they cannot be easily bought or sold on a stock exchange. Investors should be prepared for extended holding periods, as exits may take several years.

2. Market and Economic Sensitivity: Private equity performance is influenced by economic cycles and market conditions. Economic downturns can impact the valuation and profitability of portfolio companies.

3. Limited Information Access: Private companies are not subject to the same disclosure requirements as public companies. This limited access to information poses challenges for investors in conducting thorough due diligence.

4. Management Risk: The success of a private equity investment often depends on the effectiveness of the management team. Inadequate management decisions or unexpected challenges can affect the performance of the investment.

How to Invest in Private Equity

1. Direct Investments

Angel Investing: Individuals can invest directly in early-stage startups as angel investors. This approach requires a high level of risk tolerance and industry expertise.

Venture Capital Funds: Investing in venture capital funds allows individuals to gain exposure to a diversified portfolio of startups managed by experienced fund managers.

2. Private Equity Funds

Limited Partnerships: Most private equity investments involve limited partnerships, where investors become limited partners in a fund. Fund managers, acting as general partners, make investment decisions and manage the fund's operations.

Fund Selection: Investors can choose from a variety of private equity funds based on factors such as the fund's strategy, industry focus, and track record. Due diligence is crucial in evaluating a fund's performance and alignment with the investor's objectives.

3. Secondary Market

Investing in Existing Funds: Investors can gain exposure to private equity by purchasing existing fund interests on the secondary market.

This provides an opportunity to access mature funds with established portfolios.

4. Co-Investments

Direct Participation: Some private equity funds offer co-investment opportunities, allowing investors to directly participate in specific deals alongside the fund. Co-investing can enhance returns and provide a more hands-on approach to investment.

Key Considerations for Private Equity Investors

1. Risk Appetite and Investment Horizon

Investors should assess their risk tolerance and investment horizon before venturing into private equity. The illiquid nature of these investments requires a long-term commitment.

2. Due Diligence

Thorough due diligence is essential when selecting private equity funds or direct investments. This involves evaluating the fund manager's track record, investment strategy, and the financial health of portfolio companies.

3. Diversification

Diversifying across multiple private equity investments can mitigate risk. Allocating capital to different strategies, stages, and industries helps build a well-rounded private equity portfolio.

4. Alignment of Interests

Investors should seek an alignment of interests with fund managers. Understanding fee structures, performance incentives, and the manager's commitment to the fund are critical factors.

5. Regulatory Compliance

Investors must be aware of regulatory requirements governing private equity investments in their jurisdiction. Compliance with securities laws and other regulations is paramount.

Conclusion

Private equity investing offers a unique avenue for investors to actively participate in the growth and development of private companies. While the potential for high returns is enticing, it comes with inherent risks and challenges that demand careful consideration. Whether through direct investments, private equity funds, or co-investments, individuals can strategically integrate private equity into their investment portfolios.

Understanding the nuances of private equity, conducting thorough due diligence, and aligning investments with personal objectives are crucial steps toward unlocking the opportunities and navigating the complexities of this dynamic investment landscape. As investors embrace the potential rewards of private equity, a balanced and informed approach becomes the cornerstone of success in this ever-evolving financial domain.

Part 3: Success - Self

Introduction

What a man can be, he must be.

Kurt Goldstein

In this stage, we explore the meaning of true success beyond traditional ideas and delve into the concept of super success, which we define as the *ultimate success*. At this point, success takes on a very personal meaning that includes mastering the basics and achieving unparalleled levels of prosperity.

Understanding Ultimate Success

Success means different things to different people. It's about achieving personal goals and making a positive impact on society. When someone reaches the highest level of success, they feel fulfilled and happy beyond their wildest dreams. This level of success is not just about achieving goals, but also about finding a deeper connection to one's purpose in life. It's about realizing one's full potential and accomplishing what was set out to be done. Ultimately, success is about reaching a point where one feels content and satisfied with their life.

Self-Actualization

To achieve ultimate success, one must strive for *self-actualization* and surpass their wildest dreams. This involves reaching the highest level of one's craft and achieving the most significant status in a chosen field. To reach this pinnacle, one must overcome various challenges in different areas, such as conquering limiting beliefs, pursuing fitness and health goals, and attaining a certain level of wealth. This satisfaction goes beyond just doing what one was meant to do. It satisfies the innate need for significance and growth.

The Intersection of Abundance, Confidence, and Ego Dissolution

When someone reaches the peak of success, they experience a significant change. They feel *abundant* instead of lacking, and they become more *confident* in themselves. They stop worrying about what others think, and they become their *authentic selves*. This change happens because the individual no longer needs external validation or compares themselves to others. As a result, their *ego dissolves*, and they feel comfortable in their own skin. By shedding their ego, they gain true authenticity.

A Compassionate and Selfless Presence

When we aim for success, it's important to prioritize helpfulness and understanding over arrogance and cockiness. We should focus on actions that promote our personal growth and the well-being of others, rather than being driven solely by our egos. Being genuine and authentic is crucial to being likable and free from pretense. We need to balance fulfilling our own needs with contributing to the well-being of others.

Embracing the Essence: Unveiling the True Self

The story of *ultimate success* goes beyond the usual idea of achieving goals. It's like a piece of art made up of different parts, like finding out who you really are, being resilient, and staying dedicated. This journey needs you to overcome the obstacles inside of you and outside of you, and to grow beyond what society expects of you.

When you reach the top, you not only know who you are, but you also love the person you have become. It's not just about being successful on your own, but it's also about being part of a group that helps each other grow, make a difference in society, and live a real, authentic life.

> *In the world of ultimate success, you don't stand alone as a winner, but instead, you shine like a light, inspiring others to discover who they are and find their own path to happiness and fulfillment.*

On the road to success, we discover ourselves and help others. Success isn't just about achieving, it's about contributing to society. When we reach the top, we find personal fulfillment and a better society. We do this by being authentic and confident, and by not letting our egos get in the way.

Our success is part of a larger story, where our individual victories inspire others. It's a story of resilience, commitment, and determination. Success isn't just about us, but about making the world a better place. This journey doesn't end with success, though. It's a never-ending quest to know ourselves and help others find their way.

Chapter 8: Individual Self

Section 1: Introduction

In this section, we will look at what it means to be your *Ultimate Self* as part of living your *Ultimate Life*.

> *A man's highest happiness is found in the bestowal of benefits on those he loves; love finds its most natural and spontaneous expression in giving. The man who has nothing to give cannot fill his place as a husband or father, as a citizen, or as a man. It is in the use of material things that a man finds a full life for his body, develops his mind, and unfolds his soul. It is therefore of supreme importance to him that he should be rich.*
>
> Wallace Wattles

First, we will look at you as an individual, and what would you like to accomplish. What would you like to do, have, or become? Are you interested in riches, in giving back? Are you interested in having all the materialistic things that can come with being wealthy?

Do you want to be comfortable with who you are without any interference from your ego and without caring anything about what other people think about you and about what you are doing with your life?

Being your *ultimate self* is also about squeezing everything you can out of this thing called life. It's performing at top levels. It's about being the best at what you want to pursue. It's about your accomplishments and recognitions. Not for the sake of your ego, but for the sake of being able to measure where you are in life. He who has the most toys wins. He who has the most titles wins? He who has the most recognition wins. He who accomplished the most wins.

When you're thinking about what you want to achieve in the next 3 to 10 years, it's important to aim high. Set your goals at least 10 times higher than what you think is possible. Instead of just aiming for $1 million, set your sights on $10 million. And why stop there? Why not aim for $100 million? Bill Gates once envisioned a future where every household had a computer. Today, most households have multiple computers, smartphones, and tablets. Elon Musk is working toward sending humans to Mars. Setting ambitious goals leads to great accomplishments.

Unlocking the Blueprint of Human Needs

Tony Robbins, a well-known life coach and motivational speaker, explores the complex world of human desires and motivations. He suggests that we are guided by six basic needs that shape the direction of our lives, influencing our actions, decisions, and overall sense of fulfillment. Understanding these needs can provide us with a roadmap to a fulfilling life.

1. Certainty/Comfort: The Anchor of Predictability

People need certainty or comfort, which makes them seek predictability in their lives. This need arises when individuals find comfort in routine activities, such as going to the same restaurants or watching familiar shows. The reason for this need is the desire for stability and security, which helps individuals feel a sense of control in an otherwise unpredictable world.

2. Uncertainty/Variety: Embracing the Spice of Life

People seek variety because it adds excitement to their life. Although certainty brings stability, uncertainty is necessary for a fulfilling existence. Travel and new experiences are often sought after because they provide a dose of unpredictability that prevents monotony. Without variety, life can become dull and unfulfilling, causing the human spirit to yearn for change.

3. Significance: The Quest for Personal Importance

People need recognition and importance, which is called significance. They want to feel special and valued for what they do. This desire motivates them to make a difference in the world and leave a legacy that will prove their worth.

4. Love & Connection: The Essence of Shared Experiences

People have a fundamental need for love and connection, which goes beyond individual accomplishments. This need highlights the importance of having meaningful relationships and shared experiences. Simply achieving personal goals is not enough if there is no one to share those successes with. The bonds formed through love and connection are crucial for emotional well-being and a sense of belonging.

5. Growth: The Imperative of Continuous Evolution

Humans have a natural desire to improve themselves and acquire new knowledge and skills. It's important to keep growing because if you're not improving, you're falling behind. Growth is a dynamic force that helps individuals evolve and adapt to life's constantly changing landscape.

6. Contribution: Making a Meaningful Impact

To truly feel fulfilled, we must move beyond our personal goals and desires and strive to make a positive impact. This is where the need for contribution comes in. We have an innate desire to be part of something bigger than ourselves and to know that our actions are making a difference. By contributing to the world around us, we can achieve a sense of purpose that goes beyond our own individual existence.

The Interplay of Needs: Shaping Life's Trajectory

By understanding and valuing the six basic needs that drive human motivations, we gain insights into the direction of our lives, including our choices, relationships, and pursuits. Everyone has a unique combination of these needs, which prioritizes certain ones over others, shaping their personality and life trajectory. *Tony Robbins'* exploration of these six basic needs provides a blueprint for navigating the complexities of the human experience. Certainty, variety, significance, love, growth, and contribution play an intricate role in our daily lives.

Recognizing the importance of these needs offers a roadmap to personal fulfillment and a deeper understanding of the universal forces that drive human behavior. This holistic approach to life fosters not only individual growth but also contributes positively to the collective tapestry of humanity.

Section 2: Self Actualization

Self-actualization

Self-actualization is all about having a fulfilled and *ultimate life*. It's about being all that you can be. It's about knowing what your life's purpose is and going out and doing it and making things happen for yourself.

Self-actualization is about really achieving what you were set on this earth to do, without any worry or care about what other people people think about you. This is the place where most innovators, most thinkers are when they are doing their best work or when they are creating and working on their vision.

People who have reached this level can be obsessed with what they are doing and don't care what other people think. For example, people like Steve Jobs gave the world an iPod music device before we even knew we wanted one. He was described as being obsessed with whatever he was working on. Or the *Wright* brothers who introduced the world to manned flight when everyone thought they were crazy.

Self-esteem

Self-esteem is about confidence. Doing something and knowing that you are fully prepared for the task. If you are nervous and lack confidence, then you won't feel that you are ready. Self-esteem and confidence usually come from preparedness and practice. Most people aren't very confident when they are doing something for the first time or when they are fairly new at something and haven't had a lot of practice. They only become really confident when they have mastered their craft.

Some people claim that it takes about 10,000 hours of practice to master a task. I remember taking guitar lessons and always getting really nervous to perform for my instructor at practice. But then watching him perform the same piece with ease. The difference is many more hours of practice. Some tasks take a lot longer to master than others.

Purpose

Self-actualization is about working on your life's purpose. You know that this is what you were meant to do and you are doing it to the best of your ability. And you are enjoying every minute of it or at least most of the time. This is your purpose in life. You know you have found your purpose when you just can't wait to start every day and look forward to going to work.

Most people never find their purpose in life and don't even bother looking. They are too busy living their life. They got caught up in the day-to-day activities of making a living and raising a family. Some people have just given up. I often wonder at what point in people's lives when they just don't bother to care anymore.

Still, others end up pursuing the wrong path because they were forced into it by their parents or friends. I read somewhere that 75% of Americans are unhappy at their jobs. These unhappy people are Doctors who want to become actors or Lawyers who want to become Rock Stars.

It's funny that we live in a society that creates idols out of the very people we discourage our family and friends from becoming. Not many people support someone to pursue an acting career or a singing career instead of going to university to become a doctor or lawyer.

Others are still looking for their purpose and keep looking until their dying day. But at least these people haven't given up. This pursuit can also be fulfilling. Sometimes frustrating, but fulfilling. Don't get discouraged if you haven't found your purpose yet. It's better than living a life of lies and quiet desperation.

Self-actualization is also about knowing what you are good at and what you suck at, or, at least, what you aren't so good at. Now it doesn't mean that everything you are working on makes you feel good all the time. Sometimes you have to do some tasks that you don't want to do to get to where you want to go. But you do them anyway because you know they are part of the bigger path, part of your *purpose* and *vision*.

You also have to make sure you don't focus too much time on what you aren't good at or don't enjoy. Try and get someone else to do certain tasks so you can focus on your strengths. This is particularly important in business. For example, don't spend all your time on the day-to-day management of your business, if your strengths are sales and vice-versa.

How do you know that you are working on your purpose and that you are truly fulfilled? Here are some of the signs.

1. You work non-stop without realizing it. Sometimes working throughout the night. Sometimes without sleep. If you are upset because you have to stop and go to sleep, you are working on the right stuff. I sometimes get upset if I'm *in the zone* and I have to stop to go to the bathroom or my meal has arrived and I'm distracted by having to eat.

2. You are excited even when there are setbacks. Sometimes you get thrown a curve ball and you end up with some minor setbacks. Believe me, I have had my fair share of setbacks. I have had my house go into foreclosure, more than once; my car was almost repossessed; my phone has been shut off several times, I have had many lawsuits. Lots of fun things have happened to me. But if you get knocked down, just get up again. If you get knocked down 3 times, you have to get up 4 times.

3. You are getting a lot of negativity from others who are trying to discourage you from what you are doing, usually because they don't understand it or because they are just looking out for you and don't want to see you get hurt. It also may be because they don't want you to become more successful than them and leave their circle of *good enough*.

If you receive negativity, you should just ignore it and just keep going because you believe in what you are doing. It just means you are making progress.

Section 3: Ultimate Self

How can you achieve your *Ultimate Self*?

First, you have to determine what being your Ultimate Self means to you. And it could, and probably, will change. Look at *Arnold Schwarzenegger* or *Elon Musk*. Both have reached the highest level of achievement in multiple areas. Look at *Albert Schweitzer* or *Leonardo DaVinci*.

Now I'm not saying that you need to jump around from one dream to the next. What I am saying is that you can pivot if you find yourself unfulfilled in your current situation. Most people these days have multiple jobs and multiple careers. Gone are the days when people find a job and work at it for 35 years and then retire from that job.

The ultimate drive is pursuing something that you are really interested in and not something that has external drivers. A lot of Doctors and Lawyers hate their jobs but pursue them because of other benefits such as money, status, and title.

Find something you love and learn how to make money at it and you will never have to work another day in your life.

I'm envious of those people who knew what they wanted to do when they saw it. I don't know if it was a eureka moment for these people or if they slowly discovered something they were really interested in and that they really liked doing.

However I think, someone who knows what they want to do with their life at an early age will be a lot more likely to achieve greatness. They have more time to work at being great. That is not to say that people can't achieve greatness at any stage of their lives. Look at *Colonel Sanders* who started Kentucky Fried Chicken at the age of 62. He lived to be 90.

What is retirement? I see retirement as a reward for doing something you hated for many years. Now, I'm not saying everyone who retires worked at a job they hated. But I am saying that there are a lot of people who got comfortable with their lives and became complacent and never fought to realize their true potential. They never achieved greatness.

These people are filled with regrets. These same people are the ones who die shortly after they retire. They were not fulfilled.

Comfortable is the enemy of great
Jim Pellerin

The real fun in life is in the journey, not the destination. Trying to be great can be a lot of fun. It can have a lot of setbacks and discouragements too.

What will seeking your *Ultimate Self* mean for you? This is a question you should ask yourself.

It will bring you amazing happiness. It will bring you amazing discouragement. You will have many successes. You will have many setbacks. You will have many failures. You will get stressed and frustrated. You will experience days of pure ecstasy. You will experience days of great pain.

Pursuing greatness keeps you young. It keeps you energized and motivated. But it can also fatigue you. You have to learn how to deal with these frustrations, these roadblocks that are put in your way along your road to greatness.

There's something about seeing older people still working at work they are passionate about. It shows that they are truly fulfilled. These people could quit anytime, having achieved their highest levels of success. I'm talking about people like *Charlie Munger* and *Warren Buffet*. Multi-billionaires in their 90s. Recently, I was watching a video of a board meeting that *Charlie Munger* was chairing. You could tell he was enjoying it.

And why should these people retire? A friend of mine has one of the sharpest computer minds that I have ever seen. He keeps talking about retirement. I keep telling him he's too smart to retire. But he has lost his passion for his work.

I just finished writing a 10-year plan at the age of 64. There are lots I want to do and *miles to go before I sleep*. I'm passionate about finding my passion. If I had one wish in life it would be that I didn't need to sleep.

Look at the *Rolling Stones*. Still together, still touring and they are all in their 70s & 80s.

Look at *Roger Federer*, still a top tennis competitor at the age of 38 having won 2 grand slams only a couple of years prior.

So what is it that want to have, do, and become? What is your *Ultimate Vision*? What is your *Ultimate Purpose*? I know we talked about this in Chapter 1, but now it's time to 10X your desires. This means, whatever you thought you wanted, think again. But this time time think big. I mean really big. There's a common theme being tossed around in the business community these days telling people to multiply their goals 10 times (10X) from what they originally had. So if you were trying to reach a net worth of $10M, your new 10X goal would be $100M.

What do you want to be known for? Do you want to be an accomplished business person, a super athlete, an accomplished investor, or something else? Do you want to achieve certain recognitions such as titles like *Sir Elton John* or the *Richest Man in the World* or the *Fittest Man in the World*? I don't see these desires as coming from the ego even though they are all self-centered. They are just there to provide motivation, direction, and excitement.

I personally can't get motivated if my goals are simple or too easy. How many times have you heard someone say they want to make a million dollars? Now it's even commonplace to hear people even say $10M? But what about $100M? Now that's a goal. Years ago *Jim Carey* wrote himself a check for $10M. It was dated 10 years in the future. Ten years later he received $10M for starring in the movie Dumb and Dumber.

So go back to the goals that you set and rethink them. How would you feel if you achieved them? Are they challenging enough? Would you feel fulfilled?

Section 4: Recognition

Becoming the *Ultimate Self* means receiving a very high level of recognition. Both external and internal. Recognition can come in many forms.

> *Our deepest fear is not that we are inadequate. Our deepest fear is that we are powerful beyond measure.*
>
> Marianne Williamson

What did you become

One form of recognition is becoming something or making something of yourself. What did you achieve? Did you become a recognized expert in your field? Are you the go-to person for your area of expertise? For example, in self-help, *Tony Robbins* is considered by most to be the foremost expert in motivation and success coaching. He has coached millions of people and changed the lives of many people. But he also feeds millions of people every year through his donations.

Did you get the fame that you wanted? Did you become a famous celebrity or a person of interest? Are you asked to speak at conferences related to your expertise? Is your name synonymous with your expertise? Here are some examples: Social Media Marketing = *Gary Vaynerchuk*, Online Marketing Funnels = *Russell Brunson*, Talk Show Host = *David Letterman*, Basketball Player = *Michael Jordan*. These are some extreme examples but that's what I'm referring to ... extreme levels of success.

Many other people have achieved high levels of success in similar fields but these people I just mentioned are considered the best in the respective areas.

Do you want to become the best at what you do? Do you want fame, glory, and recognition? Do you want fame as a stepping stone to your real passion of being able to help people get what they want? Again. look at *Arnold Schwarzenegger*. He gave up millions of dollars that he could have made as an actor so that he could serve the people as *Governor of California*. People thought he was crazy but he said it was the most fulfilling thing he ever did in his life.

Who are you?

What titles, awards, or acknowledgments have you received? *Sir Richard Branson* has been knighted. Many people have received Honorary degrees for their efforts in their area. Are you the president or owner of a reputable firm? Have you been asked to sit on the board of any organizations? What titles have been bestowed upon you? Do people know who you are? Do you have a Wikipedia profile? Did you win a Nobel prize? Did you hold a high-ranking position in your job? Did you have a position in the government? What other major accomplishments have you achieved? Have you run a marathon? Do people know who you are when you walk down the street? Are you a well-known professional actor, singer, or athlete? Again, these are more extreme examples to highlight extreme success.

Being your *Ultimate Self* is about being a *super achiever*. I see it all the time. A successful doctor, head of surgery, runs marathons, has

10% body fat, and chairs several organizations. Success and high achievement are contagious and spill over into many areas of your life.

What did you get?

In some cases, money is a recognition of hard work and success. Some people see having money (being rich) as *superficial* but usually those are the people who don't have any wealth. Their attitude is that those rich people got rich by taking from other people.

Most people know who the top 2 or 3 richest people in the world are. At the time of this writing, the list usually includes *Jeff Bozos*, *Elon Musk*, and *Warren Buffet*. But these people aren't in it for the money, or at least not anymore. Not after having achieved a certain level of wealth. They enjoy what they are doing. The additional wealth was just a side benefit and a recognition for all their hard work and success. Something to measure their success by.

So what is it that you want to achieve for yourself? What kind of recognition do you want for your hard work and efforts? What level of success are you looking for? Is one of your goals to be an expert in your field? Or to achieve a certain level of success in your field. For example, I want to be worth $100M and help over 1 million people through my marketing, education, and investment products.

Do you want a fancy sports car and a big mansion or a big yacht where you can entertain famous people? Do you want to hang out and be friends with famous celebrities? There's nothing wrong with wanting these so-called materialistic things. They are prizes for all your hard work. They are more measurement tools.

Do you want to help feed the hungry and the poor? Do you want to be a philanthropist and donate time and money to a worthy cause? There is a lot of overlap with these desires as well. For example, *Bill Gates* made his billions in software as the owner of Microsoft and now he is using that money to cure diseases with his foundation. He has also recruited other rich people like *Warren Buffet* to kick in a few billion.

Another example is how some celebrities will use their *stardom* for worthwhile causes and charities. For example, Oprah Winfrey is famous for all the charities that she supports.

How would you like to make a sizable donation to your university or set up a scholarship fund in your name?

Life didn't happen to these successful people. At some point in their life, they decided that they wanted to make something of themselves and to do something with their life. A lot of these successful people struggled and persevered through adversity and obstacles but never quit. They may have re-aligned a couple of times but they became successful at what they wanted to do and have the things they wanted to have and receive the recognition they deserve.

And don't get fooled by your change in course. You may start on a journey to become one thing and end up being something else because you were better at it and it was easier and more enjoyable for you to succeed at. *Walt Disney* started out as a newspaper editor. *Harrison Ford* started as a carpenter. *Ken Jeong* was a Doctor and gave it up to be an actor (starred as *Mr. Chow* in The *Hangover*). What if these people decided not to pursue their ultimate dreams?

Chapter 9: Social Self

Section 1: Introduction

Love, relationships, and belonging are essential parts of the human experience. They connect us to others and give our lives meaning. In this section, we'll look at the different aspects of relationships, the importance of belonging, the power of love, and the health benefits that come with love and sex.

Relationships

Relationships are an essential part of human life. They can take many different forms such as family, friends, and romantic partners, and each one has a unique impact on our lives. Relationships play a significant role in shaping our emotions, behavior, and even our physical health. Good relationships can make us feel secure, supported, and emotionally healthy, while difficult relationships can lead to stress, anxiety, and negative health effects. Our connections with others are a crucial aspect of our lives as social beings. The quality of our relationships profoundly affects our overall well-being.

Belonging

Everyone wants to belong to a group. It's a basic human need that goes beyond borders, cultures, or social status. We all want to be accepted, contribute, and identify with a community. When we feel like we belong, it has a positive impact on our mental health, self-esteem, and overall life satisfaction. On the other hand, when we feel excluded and isolated, it can lead to emotional distress and negatively impact our well-being. That's why it's important to create communities that nurture the human spirit and promote a sense of belonging.

Love and Connection

Love and connection are two intertwined aspects of the human experience that shape our emotions. Love is not solely confined to romantic relationships, but extends to friendships, family, and friends. Physical and emotional connections foster a sense of intimacy and shared experiences, which contribute to emotional resilience, happiness, and an enriched life. Recognizing the different forms of love and connection highlights the diverse nature of human emotions.

Contribution

Contributing to others is an important part of building meaningful relationships. It feels good to give love and support, but giving also creates a sense of purpose and satisfaction. When we show kindness, empathy, and support, we strengthen our social connections and enrich our shared humanity. It's important to embrace the role of contributing in our relationships, not just for our own fulfillment, but for the benefit of everyone involved.

Benefits of Love and Sex

Love and sex aren't just emotional experiences; they can also have health benefits. Studies show that being in a loving relationship, physically touching, and having sex can all improve your overall well-being. When you're intimate with someone, your body releases oxytocin, which is sometimes called the *love hormone*. This chemical can help reduce stress and strengthen emotional connections. Additionally, regular sexual activity can have cardiovascular benefits, showing that physical health and intimate relationships are closely related.

In summary, human connection is central to our well-being. Relationships, love, belonging, and giving back are all important parts of life. Understanding the significance of these elements can help us lead happier, healthier lives. As social beings, we all benefit from strong connections with others. By recognizing the importance of these relationships, we can help create a more connected world.

Let's explore these concepts in more detail.

Section 2: Relationships

One of the characteristics of being an *Ultimate Social* person is the relationships you have with the people around you. This includes family, friends, colleagues, etc. This is all about how you treat these people and how you interact with these people. Let's look at different types of people that you should be socializing with.

Child to Your Parents

Are your parents still around? If you are that fortunate, then you want to make the best of the time you have left with them. Do you try and see them often? How is your relationship with them? Do you include them in your own family activities? Do you treat them with the respect they deserve? Make sure you spend as much time with your parents as you both would like.

People tend to ignore their parents when they leave their birth home and start a family of their own. They get busy. They also end up regretting it later in life when they wish they had spent more time with them. Maybe have a weekly call and get together more for dinner and special occasions. If your relationship is not good and you want to fix it, then take the time to do so. If the differences are too much, then just move on. Ultimately, it's your decision.

Husband / Wife to your Spouse or Partner

Just because you are married doesn't mean the passion has to fade. And just because you have a family and you both work don't think you can't make time for each other. This is why most marriages fail. That and financial issues, but later on finance.

You both work hard all day, you come home spend some time running around with the kids and then you are tired and go to bed. Try to spend a little bit of time each day with your partner, even if it's just to sit in front of the TV together for 30 minutes to watch Jeopardy (about the only show I watch).

You should also have at least one night a week together. This could be alone or with friends. Just because you are married, doesn't mean you have to stop being friends. You usually end up getting married because you met your best friend. Don't let work, family, and life get in the way of that and break up your friendship.

Mother / Father / Parent to Your Children

Are you are mother or father? Do you have children? How do you treat your children? Do you spend time with them? Are you there for them when you need to be? Do you provide them with the guidance they need? You need to be strict but not controlling. You also need to be fair and let them learn for themselves. Do you plan family outings? When was the last time you went on a vacation together? Make sure you allocate time to spend with your children. Children are influenced greatly by the people they spend time with. Make sure one of those people is you. Try to spend as much time with them as you can. They will appreciate it.

Brother / Sister to your Siblings.

If you have siblings, you should still try and make time for them. If you still live in the same city it's a lot easier. This doesn't have to be as often as your immediate family but should still be as frequent as you both would like. What about having a BBQ once a month or inviting them over for your children's special days, like birthdays, graduations, etc?

Friends

Being an *Ultimate Social* person means you have friends that you see regularly. These are people you have common interests with, whether it be sports or entertainment or maybe even business-related. In my real estate investing days, there were a lot of people that I used to see at special events and that I would socialize with.

If you are meeting at special events you should hang out with these people before or after the events. Don't lock yourself in your hotel room. If they are friends you know from outside of your business circles, you might go to sporting activities together, dinners, or concerts.

Co-worker

A relationship with a co-worker is an interesting one. The more time you spend with a co-worker, the more you get to know them, and the more you can enjoy their company. Or you may ultimately decide you don't want to have a relationship with that person. You may decide that you don't have any interests in common and you spend as little time with those people as possible. And that's OK. For the people you do like, you may develop a deeper friendship that could last for years or even a lifetime.

I remember when I started my first job, I moved to another city. Most of the people at this job were new and were also from other cities. We did everything together. Dinners, pub nights, house parties, bike trips, birthday parties, etc. We had weekly events where we could always count on seeing each other and having a good time. It was a great experience to have that many new friends right out of university.

University was another great place to make friends and socialize. I really enjoyed my social life at University. Maybe a bit too much ... haha.

The important point to take from this section is that life is all about the company you keep and the moments you spend with people. Don't spend all your time working or alone at home watching TV. People get caught up with life and don't take the time to enjoy it with other people. Force yourself to attend those family social events, especially if you are single and without children. You never know who you are going to meet. You will never hear anyone saying they regret having spent too much time with their family and they should have spent more time at the office or watching TV. You worked hard to achieve *Ultimate Success*. Make sure you reap the benefits from all your hard work and that you can spend time with friends and loved ones.

I saw a documentary recently about the long-term friendship between *Don Rickles* and *Bob Newhart* and their wives. Friends for over 60 years. Very touching.

Section 3: Social Clubs

Part of having an *Ultimate Life* and having an *Ultimate Social* life is being a valued member of society and participating in community social events. This includes such things as community fundraisers, business clubs, volunteer organizations, sports clubs, etc. It means giving back and helping out with the community and also having some fun. All work and no play is not a good approach to your *Ultimate Life*.

Social groups

There are many social organizations which you can belong to if you so desire. These clubs range from fundraising clubs, sports clubs, luncheon groups, etc. They come in many forms and usually meet regularly or as needed. An example of these groups is the *Lions Club International* which is a social group that helps people throughout the world. Their main focus is fundraising for worthwhile causes. There are also private organizations that are set up to help specific causes. Maybe you might want to start one of your own.

One way to find some of these groups is to check out *meetup.com*. They have many different meetings on just about any topic you can imagine in your area. You can go and learn about real estate, talk about movies, learn how to set up a business, participate in a sports event, or even go on bike rides together. There are many areas of interest for you to check out. It just depends on how active you want to be and what you want to achieve.

Fund Raising Groups

There are many fundraising groups that you can partake in. The nice thing about belonging to a fundraising group is that it allows you to give back. For example, a lot of executives who retire get involved in organizations like the *United Way* whose main function is to raise money for worthwhile causes. *United Way* usually has companies pledging a certain amount of money that they will raise.

By heading up one of these initiatives, you can stay active in the business world but not have to worry about the day-to-day hustle of actually doing the business. Search out a fundraising organization that resonates with you and join up.

Hospitals are always looking for people to volunteer in some capacity. Or maybe you want to start your *own* foundation or fundraising organization to support a worthwhile cause that has affected you and your family. Look at the amazing work that the *Bill and Melinda Gates Foundation* is doing. Look at the awareness that the *Mothers Against Drunk Drivers (MADD)* has brought to driving while impaired. I have always wanted to start a fundraising initiative to help raise money to promote the advancement of education in my hometown, and to help promote people to start their own businesses. Sort of like an incubation center.

Volunteer Boards

Have you reached a certain level of success and you would now like to share the knowledge that you have acquired that has provided you with that success? One of the ways you can do this is by volunteering to sit on a board as a director for a volunteer or non-profit organization. If you are a recognized expert in your field, I'm sure communities would welcome your participation as a board member.

Maybe you can help out a startup company or someone who's looking at getting into business and your area of expertise would help them. Maybe you could become a mentor to some business people looking to get started. Sometimes it's more the general business knowledge that you contribute rather than the specific domain expertise, such as *internet marketing* or *real estate investing*, which would be the case for me.

Business clubs

I used to belong to a private members club. This was a nice place to go and relax and meet with some like-minded individuals. I don't know if I ever received any business as a result of my being a member, but it was certainly a good social atmosphere. I would eat lunch there once or twice a week with some of the local business owners. I would also attend any special social events that they would have throughout the year. For example, I attended the 1999 New Year's Eve party and several annual holiday events such as St Patrick's Day party, Easter Brunch, etc.

The big difference between this type of club and the fundraising club is that you usually just have to pay an annual membership and then just show up for these events. You don't have to really do any work or volunteer any of your time unless you want to sit on the board of one of these clubs. Being a member of one of these elite business clubs is also a recognition of a certain status level that you have achieved. These clubs can be very expensive and usually require a minimum spend limit at their restaurants and bars. The advantage is you get to hang out with some very accomplished people and can have some really interesting conversations and trade stories.

Sports Clubs

Being a member of a local sports club is also very common. You could join a golf club, a racket or tennis club, a bowling or dart league, etc. There are lots of these clubs and they range in price and participation.

Some golf clubs require an initiation fee of $100,000 or more just to join. Then they require you to pay a yearly membership fee and have a guaranteed meal and drink spend requirement. These facilities are quite lavish and very exclusive. Again, the big advantage is you get to meet some very prominent people and you can have some very good conversations with like-minded individuals.

At the other end of the spectrum, you can choose to join a bowling or dart league, if that's what you would prefer. Usually, there's no membership fee and sometimes they are even sponsored by a local business. Neither of these types of clubs is better or worse, they are just different and it all depends on what you would enjoy. I know of some very rich people who prefer to go out to a local pub for beer and chicken wings and hate the idea of champagne and caviar. Just because you have achieved wealth, doesn't mean you have to spend it on expensive things, especially if you don't like those things.

Section 4: Philanthropy

Philanthropy is not only about giving money to charitable causes, but also about helping others selflessly through financial support, donating time, and using one's influence to improve society. *Bill and Melinda Gates* are prime examples of modern philanthropists who have dedicated their time and wealth to tackle diseases and global challenges. Everyone, regardless of their financial status or age, can become a philanthropist if they have a genuine desire to make a positive impact on the lives of others. Effective philanthropy demands commitment, strategic thinking, and a willingness to care for others beyond oneself. It is not just about writing a check, but about helping in various ways to make a real difference.

You can become a philanthropist by giving away your time, money, or even your reputation if you have a well-recognized and respected reputation. It means you would care for someone else's needs and not just your own. Being a philanthropist is a very rewarding endeavor and should not be taken lightly.

Philanthropy is usually something people wait to do once they retire. But it doesn't have to be that way. A lot of people have begun way before then. They may start small and then ramp up once they retire and have more time. Being a philanthropist can be very rewarding because you get to help others.

The key to being a good philanthropist is that you want to take it seriously and treat it just like you would a job. You want to be smart about it. You want to be successful at it. Here are a few things that you should be doing.

1. Create a Strategy - Before you begin anything, you want to make sure you have an overall strategy. What is going to be your approach? Will you be doing this part-time or full-time? Are you going to focus on one or many initiatives? Are you going to be giving money or just your time or both? Are you looking to start your own initiative or would you like to help out one of the many that are already initiatives out there? What type of project would you be interested in working on? I have always wanted to start a type of incubation center where I help early startups get started. Maybe I will.

2. Do your research - There are lots of existing foundations and initiatives that you could help out with. And they focus on many different areas. For example, you could help with world hunger or poverty or the environment or something to do with animals. Or maybe you want to start your own foundation and help people in your hometown. Maybe you want to set up a scholarship in your name or maybe donate money to build a new library or fitness facility. You could help promote a particular sport. Maybe you want to set up an annual fund-raising event by relating it to sports. For example, look at all the money the *Terry Fox Foundation* has raised for cancer research.

3. Look for sustainable solutions - You will want to choose something that has been around for a long time so that you know it has been effective. For example, *United Way*, *UNICEF*, and the *World Wildlife Federation* are long-term foundations that have helped millions of people for many years. You also will want to make sure that you aren't going to help something that won't be around for a long time. Unless, of course, the goal is to complete it in the near future.

4. Learn to lead - I'm assuming you are a successful person and have become so as a result of your ability to lead others. You will need to leverage your leadership skills and apply them to your philanthropy efforts. Most people are wanting to help but are looking for some type of direction. They don't mind pitching in but don't want the added responsibility of decision-making that can come with leading something.

5. Volunteer - Now it's time to execute your strategy. You can volunteer your time, donate and contribute your money, or lend your reputation. You can decide whether to be active or passive. You can lead or participate. You may also want to get other people to participate in your cause. Again, you can get people to help and to contribute in whatever capacity they want giving your time or money or both.

6. Re-evaluate - After a while, you may want to re-evaluate your philanthropy efforts. How do you think your initiatives are progressing? Are you happy with the results? Do you want to make changes in which projects you are helping? Do you want to add, change, or delete a project? Do you want to increase or decrease the amount of time and effort that you are putting into this? Do you want to change the direction of the types of projects you are helping?

Becoming a philanthropist can be a life-changing and fulfilling experience that goes beyond traditional charitable giving. It involves taking a well-rounded approach, which includes giving time, resources, and influence to make a significant difference. Anyone can contribute, no matter their age or stage in life. By being strategic, conducting research, and actively participating in chosen causes, one can maximize the impact of their philanthropic efforts. It's not just about giving once, but about consistently reevaluating strategies to ensure sustained effectiveness and adaptability to changing societal needs. Philanthropy, when approached with dedication and purpose, can be a powerful force for positive change, leaving behind a legacy that extends far beyond personal accomplishments.

Conclusion

In conclusion, the framework presented in this book offers a structured approach to achieving your goals and realizing your *ultimate life* vision. By defining your purpose and setting SMART goals that are specific, measurable, achievable, relevant, and time-bound, you can create a roadmap for success. It is crucial to identify and overcome any limiting beliefs that may be holding you back, as these can hinder your progress towards your aspirations. Aligning your actions with your goals and staying focused on the desired results are key components of this framework.

Success is not solely defined by material possessions or professional accomplishments; it encompasses building strong social connections, fostering a sense of belonging, and positively impacting the lives of others. By nurturing these essential aspects of life, you can create a more fulfilling and meaningful existence. Embracing your purpose and setting meaningful goals that resonate with your ultimate vision are foundational steps towards achieving ultimate success. Taking purposeful action and remaining open to receiving the outcomes of your efforts are essential elements in this journey.

Overcoming fears and limiting beliefs is a critical aspect of personal growth and development. By challenging yourself to step outside your comfort zone and confront obstacles head-on, you can unlock new levels of potential and achieve greater success. Remember that success is a holistic pursuit that involves continuous learning, adaptation, and self-improvement. By cultivating a growth mindset and embracing challenges as opportunities for growth, you can navigate life's complexities with resilience and determination.

As you progress on your path towards ultimate success, stay committed to your goals and remain adaptable to changing circumstances. Embrace setbacks as learning experiences and use them to refine your approach and strategies. By staying true to your values and aspirations, you can create a life that reflects your deepest desires and aspirations. Success is not a destination but a continuous journey of self-discovery and personal evolution.

In the pursuit of ultimate success, it is essential to cultivate a sense of purpose and direction that guides your actions and decisions. By staying focused on your long-term vision and breaking down your goals into actionable steps, you can make steady progress towards your desired outcomes. Remember that success is a multifaceted concept that encompasses not only personal achievements but also contributions to the greater good.

By fostering strong social connections and nurturing relationships with others, you can create a support system that sustains you on your journey towards success. Surround yourself with individuals who uplift and inspire you, and reciprocate that positivity by offering support and encouragement to others. Success is not a solitary endeavor but a collaborative effort that thrives on mutual growth and empowerment.

As you navigate the complexities of life and work towards your ultimate goals, maintain a sense of gratitude for the opportunities and experiences that come your way. Cultivate a mindset of abundance and appreciation for the blessings in your life, and use that positivity to fuel your drive towards success. By acknowledging and celebrating your achievements, no matter how small, you can build momentum and confidence in your abilities.

In conclusion, achieving ultimate success requires a holistic approach that integrates personal growth, professional development, and social contribution. By following the framework outlined in this book and staying true to your values and aspirations, you can create a life that is rich in meaning and purpose. Embrace challenges as opportunities for growth, and view setbacks as stepping stones towards greater achievements. Remember that success is a journey, not a destination, and stay committed to continuous learning and self-improvement.

As you embark on the next phase of your journey towards ultimate success, remember to stay focused on your goals, remain adaptable to change, and cultivate a mindset of resilience and determination. By embodying these qualities and staying true to your vision, you can overcome obstacles and achieve your desired outcomes. Success is within your reach; all it takes is dedication, perseverance, and a willingness to embrace the journey with an open heart and mind.

Check out WWW.JIMPELLERIN.COM[1] for more articles by Jim Pellerin

1. http://WWW.JIMPELLERIN.COM

About The Author

JIM PELLERIN started real estate investing over twenty years ago. Since then, he has bought and sold millions of dollars of real estate. He began by purchasing and renting out duplexes. Recently he has added Lease Options to his strategy. He is currently acquiring two to four Lease Option properties a month. He has implemented many unique funding strategies that have allowed him to continue implementing his strategy and continue building his sizable portfolio.

As part of his education, he has attended numerous seminars on real estate investing, project management, property management, financing, renovations, motivation, time management, and many more. He has also read over 500 books on similar topics.

This book blends his experience and the knowledge he has gained through his investments and studies.

Visit his author page to discover my other publications: books2read.com/JimPellerin[1]

1. https://books2read.com/JimPellerin

Other Books By Jim Pellerin

Real Estate Investing: Strategies – The Secret to Financial Independence with Real Estate

books2read.com/strategies[1]

1. https://books2read.com/strategies

Real Estate Investing with Lease Options – How to Invest with No Money Down

books2read.com/Lease-Options[2]

2. https://books2read.com/Lease-Options

Invest NOW – The Passive Approach to Winning with Real Estate

books2read.com/investnow[3]

3. https://books2read.com/investnow

books2read.com/JimPellerin[4]

4. https://books2read.com/JimPellerin

Did you love *Life Now - The Ultimate Life Framework*? Then you should read *Invest Now - The Passive Approach to Winning at Real Estate*[5] by Jim Pellerin!

[6]

People are lost when it comes to investing and planning for their retirement. The stock market is underperforming and has always been volatile. And besides who has the time to learn enough to invest in the right companies?

Real estate investing has long been an investment alternative for many people over the years. But most people don't know how to get started in real estate. And most people think real estate is risky and takes a lot of time and so people shy away from it.

But what if there was a way to make money with real estate without having to invest any of your own time *"Passive Real Estate Investing"*

---

5. https://books2read.com/u/3nDl89

6. https://books2read.com/u/3nDl89

is the solution. You can invest in real estate almost like you would invest in the stock market. *Invest NOW* covers everything you need to know to decide if passive real estate investing is the right investment alternative for you. Real estate investing doesn't have to be hard, as long as you are informed.

Jim Pellerin has been investing in real estate for over 25 years. He has been involved in over $30M of real estate transactions and has done over 100 deals. His experience covers many different real estate strategies including buy rent and hold. fix and flip. rent to own. development projects and mortgage lending. Jim is also the author of *Real Estate Investing - The Secret to Financial Independence with Real Estate* and *Real Estate Investing - The Secret to Financial Independence with Real Estate.*

Read more at www.jimpellerin.com.

Also by Jim Pellerin

Life Now

Life Now - The Ultimate Life Framework

Invest Now - The Passive Approach to Winning at Real Estate

Real Estate Investing

Real Estate Investing Strategies: The Secret to Financial Independence with Real Estate

Real Estate Investing with Lease Options - Investing in Real Estate with No Money Down

Mastering REIT Investments - A Comprehensive Guide to Wealth Building

The Ultimate Beginners Guide to Real Estate Investing

The 98 Best Real Estate Investing Strategies

The Ultimate Beginners Guide to Wholesale Real Estate Investing

The Ultimate Beginners Guide to Rental Real Estate Investing

The Ultimate Beginners Guide to Fix and Flip Real Estate Investing

The Ultimate Beginners Guide to Private Equity Real Estate Investing

Ultimate Beginners Guide to Real Estate Investing Financing

Building Wealth Through Real Estate - A Beginners Retirement Guide

The Ultimate Guide to Marketing for Real Estate Investors

Unleashing Wealth: A Guide to BRRRR Real Estate Investing

Watch for more at www.jimpellerin.com.

About the Author

Jim Pellerin has been investing in Real Estate for over 25 years. During that time, he has conducted over $30M worth of real estate transactions.

He was the founder of several Real Estate businesses with the latest, Peller Media, focusing on providing digital marketing services for real estate professionals such as real estate agents and mortgage brokers and investors.

He has read over 700 books on subjects such as real estate investing, self development, education, cognitive psychology, marketing and sales.

He has a degree in Computer Science which he received from the University of New Brunswick in Fredericton, New Brunswick, Canada.

Read more at www.jimpellerin.com.

www.ingramcontent.com/pod-product-compliance
Lightning Source LLC
LaVergne TN
LVHW022035200926
848481LV00003B/695